Lavish Lace

Knitting with Hand-Painted Yarns

Carol Rasmussen Noble
Cheryl Potter

Martingale®
& COMPANY

Martingale & Company
20205 144th Avenue NE
Woodinville, WA 98072-8478
www.martingale-pub.com

Printed in China
09 08 07 06 05 04   8 7 6 5 4 3 2 1

Library of Congress Cataloging-in-Publication Data
Noble, Carol. R. (Carol Rasmussen)
   Lavish lace : knitting with hand-painted yarns /
Carol R. Noble and Cheryl Potter.
      p. cm.
   ISBN: 1-56477-548-8
   1. Knitted lace—Patterns. I. Potter, Cheryl. II. Title.
   TT805 .K54N63 2004
   746 .2 ' 26041—dc22
                                        2004010485

Mission Statement

Dedicated to providing quality products
and service to inspire creativity.

Credits

President: Nancy J. Martin
CEO: Daniel J. Martin
Publisher: Jane Hamada
Editorial Director: Mary V. Green
Managing Editor: Tina Cook
Technical Editor: Ursula Reikes
Copy Editor: Liz McGehee
Design Director: Stan Green
Illustrator: Robin Strobel
Cover and Text Designer: Regina Girard
Studio Photographer: Brent Kane
Fashion Photographer: John P. Hamel

Dedication

To our mothers

Acknowledgments

The work of this book would have been impossible without the teaching and encouragement of my lace mentor, Margaret Peterson, of Unst, Shetland. She collaborated on the design and production of Chancay Morning, Rainstorm and Desert Dusk, and Rosebuds and Climbing Roses. I would also like to thank the entire staff of Martingale, and Mary Green in particular, for bringing this new idea to fruition. My husband and family were a great support to me, as were Margaret Dalrymple and Claudia Judson Chesney. Thank you to Galina Alexandrovna Khmeleva for introducing me to lace.
                                        —Carol Rasmussen Noble

I want to thank everyone involved for making this collaboration possible. First, my coauthor Carol Noble and of course the visionaries at Martingale, especially Karen Soltys and my technical editor, Ursula Reikes. Specialty mills around the country and abroad were especially helpful regarding sample production of new and exciting yarns. Writing this book would not have been possible without the tireless support of my employees here at Cherry Tree Hill Inc. and my family and friends. Thank you all, and enjoy!
                                        —Cheryl Potter

Contents

From the Designer's Perspective

By Carol Rasmussen Noble

LACE KNITTING IS MY PASSION. When I began to learn lace knitting from my mentor, Margaret Peterson, of Unst, Shetland, I started with the complete set of misconceptions that haunt every beginning lace knitter: I thought of fine yarns and small needles that are difficult to handle, incomprehensible directions, the slow and tedious nature of the work, and the limited design possibilities. But as I progressed, Margaret, arguably the best traditional Shetland lace knitter alive, set me straight. My ideas were too rigid. She encouraged me to experiment, which opened a door to pure knitting joy.

I want to share this joy with all knitters. I want to open this same door for them so that they can see, as I did, that lace is for everyone. Throw out those preconceived ideas! Lace knitting is pure freedom. It is a state of mind, an approach to knitting that is accessible to all knitters, no matter what their skill levels or tastes. Lace can be knitted in almost any kind of yarn with any size needles and, most important, in an infinite range of glorious colors.

Keep in mind that this book is designed in a lesson-plan format. To best use this book and to best learn to knit lace, you should knit the projects in order, starting with Ocean Moods and working your way through each one to the last project, Frost Flowers.

This book teaches a nontraditional approach in a range of projects that combine traditional Shetland and Icelandic patterns, simple techniques, helpful hints, and an extraordinary palette of colorways and textures. The "Learning Curve," "Technical Tips," and "Beginner's Edge" sections provide you with the information you need to complete each lace project. This is a something-for-everyone book, an introduction to a new world.

Why the scarves and shawls? They are easy to design and make, they lend themselves to color and texture, and they require only a small investment in time and money. And on top of this, they are also fashion statements! Why hand-painted variegated yarns? Because they have so much to give. My foundations as a designer are complex color and making complex color accessible. I have a vision that I very much wish to share: that you do not have to knit lace in all white, and you do not have to dress in all pastel, all muted, or all naturals unless you wish to. There is nothing wrong with these options; I only emphasize that they are not mandatory. There is complete freedom to choose. Fortunately, we as knitters now find ourselves in a world where there are myriad variegated yarns available, and I hope knitters will feel free to explore them in lace.

Cheryl Potter is a brilliant colorist who has always supplied me with exquisite colorways and fibers no matter what kind of knitting I am doing. I feel that by combining our talents we have produced some magnificent projects. Nevertheless, my approach can be used with any hand-painted colorway that the knitter chooses, and there are many yarns out there to select from. I call this approach the "potluck" approach. You see a variegated yarn that you like—you are drawn to it; it has something to say—and you give it voice. Each colorway, each fiber says something different to each knitter. Learn to trust your listening!

From the Fiber Artist's Perspective

By Cheryl Potter

I AM A COLORIST. The interplay of color and fiber excites me. When I began to dye yarn years ago, I bought plain, mill-end cotton and wool from local mills in New England. I mistakenly thought the point of painted yarn was to control just one design variable, an idea that resulted in smooth yarns with variegated colors. I had much to learn.

Fortunately, I discovered yarn dealers who could provide me with exotic fibers such as silk, alpaca, and cashmere. Imagine my excitement: I found that various fibers took dyes differently, and if the fiber had texture—for example, a bouclé or a plied yarn with a fancy binder—the result was more interesting still. This kind of experimentation still fascinates me as I layer color and texture and fiber to produce depth and complexity. Each new colorway is painted in at least fifty different fibers and blends. I am fond of saying "all yarns, all colorways," no matter what the fiber content, texture, or original shade of the yarn.

Soon I started to design yarn. Creating exotic fiber blends is satisfying because it gives the fiber artist yet another variable to consider in the design process. When I began painting lace yarns, I had many of the common preconceived notions. I thought lace had a little niche somewhere, but it was certainly not anything for which I would care to paint yarns. I visualized fussy little hanks purchased singly, because of the extraordinary yardage of lace-weight yarn, and then only by a very few yarn shops run by octogenarians. Wrong again.

My wake-up call came as I visited a mill in New Zealand and saw the kilos and kilos of lace-weight yarn being sold. I decided to try some merino lace and some exotic lace yarn milled from Possum. The Possum lace found its way into just about every knitting magazine possible, and lace knitters seemed to pour out of the woodwork, clamoring for more exotic fiber. One of them was Carol Noble, someone who was to become a friend and collaborator. As we began to work on projects together, it became a challenge to find designs for certain yarns, or yarns for certain designs. Carol kept pushing the lace envelope, urging me to create a wider range of yarn for lace, confident that lace knitters everywhere wanted what I was already trying to provide the rest of the knitting world: texture, color, and exotic fiber. My belief has always been that hand-painted yarns are not just for knitters who can afford fine fibers; hand-painted yarns are for everyone.

Knitted Lace Basics

What You Need to Know to Start Knitting Lace

Following are some basic principles you need to be aware of and master before beginning your first lace project.

Gauge Swatch

To create a gauge swatch, cast on the number of stitches needed to complete a repeat in the pattern motif, plus beginning and ending stitches. Ideally, a swatch of about 4" square provides enough area to calculate accurate finished measurements. Knit the swatch in the pattern stitch, with garter edges, for two to three vertical repeats or more if you need additional length. It is important to keep track of how many horizontal and vertical repeats you complete and to bind off loosely.

Now measure the width of the swatch and divide that figure into the number of horizontal stitches. This gives you the unblocked stitches per inch. Next, measure the length of the swatch and then divide this figure into the number of rows you have knit. This gives you the unblocked rows per inch. Hint: To easily and accurately count stitches and rows, simply take the number of repeats and multiply by the number of stitches or rows in each repeat; then add the beginning and ending stitches or rows for the total.

A blocked gauge swatch provides the most reliable measurement in any knitted piece. To block the swatch, first soak it in cold water overnight and then press it in a towel to remove excess moisture. Pin it out on a flat surface until taut, stretching it as much as possible. Lace dries quickly, and in just a few hours you can unpin the swatch and repeat the simple math described above to calculate the blocked gauge. As a small example of the dimensions of the finished garment after blocking, the gauge swatch can save hours of time by preventing sizing errors. From the swatch, it is easy to extrapolate how many stitches to cast on and rows to knit to create a finished piece of given dimensions. When working with sizing in lace, remember that finished measurements always refer to blocked garments.

Needles

For knitting lace, I recommend using short, straight needles 8" to 10" long. They are easy to maneuver, and you do not have to worry about balancing the weight of too-long needles. Circular needles are not optimum, because they make it difficult to maintain proper tension since the needle point and wire or plastic connector have different circumferences. Lacework requires a flexible needle with a strong, tapered point to manipulate the yarn successfully. I prefer Bryspun needles, which have long points and are very flexible. Another viable option is bamboo needles. Metal needles are usually not appropriate, as they do not grip the stitches well enough and tend to lose yarn overs; some yarns, however, do work better with metal needles. Although hardwoods have sufficient grip, they are totally inflexible and will break under even slight pressure to bend. If you can't find, or don't want to invest in, needles that are short enough, you can make a set with two double-pointed needles by putting a stopper or rubber band on one end of each needle.

Slipped Edge Stitches

In almost all lace knitting, the first stitch of every row is slipped, unless otherwise indicated in the pattern. This provides an even, stretchy edge that is vital to lace knitting. This is also a must when stitches are to be picked up along an edge later.

To work the edge stitch, slip the first stitch purlwise with the yarn in front, and then take the yarn from front to back to prepare to knit the next stitch.

Tension

Tension in lacework may vary depending upon the yarn, but it must be even across the piece, no matter what. Contrary to popular belief, most lacework requires moderate to tight tension. If you are working with an unfamiliar yarn, test tension on your gauge swatch and then block it to see which tension looks best. Stitches and yarn overs should not be allowed to become loopy, especially on small needles. In general, tighter is better.

Counting Rows and Stitches

It is important to keep track of stitches and rows so that you know exactly where you are in the pattern. Placing markers is helpful. I wear a counter on a string around my neck. If you put a counter on the end of a needle, then the two needles are no longer evenly balanced or equal in weight and your knitting will reflect this discrepancy. If I need to count both rows and stitches, I wear two counters on the string around my neck.

Colorway Considerations

Running color and texture at the same time can be tricky. We recommend choosing which you would rather feature before beginning a project. When considering colorways for specific lace projects, recall that most lace motifs are small and sometimes busy. Unless you have a very simple pattern, we suggest forgoing a high-contrast colorway, which can detract from the pattern stitch. Monochromatic colorways are perfect for fancy lace motifs, while space-dyed colorways and hand-painted hanks work wonders for simple knit-purl stitch patterns. Remember that with hand-painted yarns, it is fine to let the yarn do the work!

Learning through Swatching

Accompanying each project in this book you will find a discussion of swatches in yarns that are different from the project yarn. Some of these yarns will be identified as unsuitable. You may find this unusual in a knitting book, but I have a clear purpose in mind. The swatches are teaching examples, shown to help you learn how various lace yarns in different fibers and colorways will respond in different types of patterns and garments. I'm showing you ahead of time some of the pitfalls, so you can avoid making those mistakes yourself. There are many kinds of lace yarn; in fact, any yarn can be used for lace. The key is to learn which yarn to use for which pattern, so you achieve the look you want in the finished garment. The whole discussion of yarns and swatches is results-oriented. I want you to have enough information to make your own yarn and color choices, so that the book is a learning tool that helps you successfully create *your own lace.*

Designing the Project

BY CAROL RASMUSSEN NOBLE

PICTURE WITH ME a rare sunny day on the northernmost Shetland Isle—Unst. The seas glitter in the sunshine. But the seas are deep and rough and treacherous here where the North Sea meets the North Atlantic. Colors are a swirl of deep greens, blues, turquoises, and purples. Cheryl's colorway Tropical Storm was a natural choice for this vision.

The design I selected to represent my ocean mood is Shetland Crest o' the Wave, a beginner motif with an easy repeat in garter stitch. The stitch pattern lends itself easily to a directional scarf. This means that the project is knit from one end to the other and that the two ends will be slightly different because the pattern runs one

way. Another nice feature that complements the simplicity of the scarf is that it is self-scalloping, meaning that it finishes itself at both ends. The resultant garment requires very little blocking and drapes beautifully.

The yarn Cheryl found for me to complete the mood was Cascade Fingering Silk. I selected this yarn only after I had swatched various yarns in similar ocean colorways. While these yarns and colors may be appropriate for other projects, Cascade worked best for this introductory project on several levels.

Cascade Fingering Silk is a two-ply, 100% cultivated silk yarn, and I chose the thicker fingering-weight version rather than the traditional lace-weight version. This slightly thicker weight is easier to handle, and the silk gives the yarn plenty of stick on the needle. The yarn has a tight twist with no stretch in the fiber, so tension problems are not an issue for the knitter. This is vital, because a person who is knitting lace for the first time needs to learn the feel of making lace stitches without having to focus on tension.

Although the yarn used in Ocean Moods is finer than what many knitters are familiar with and the needles are smaller, this user-friendly yarn ensures a successful first project. Cascade is an exciting yarn to knit. It refracts light brilliantly to create highlights within highlights in the body of the knitted piece, an example of what hand painters call letting the yarn do the work for the knitter. With this yarn, even the simplest project becomes a work of wearable art!

DESIGNING THE TROPICAL STORM COLORWAY

BY CHERYL POTTER

My inspiration for the colorway Tropical Storm was a monsoon I witnessed in the Virgin Islands. The storm overtook the sunny turquoise sky in a roiling mass of gray and purple, sending torrents of rain over the tranquil island of St. John and causing an immediate flash flood that lasted only a few minutes. The sudden fury of the monsoon left me sodden and speechless, so for expression I turned to the use of color. The dangerous wonder of a tropical storm is easy to translate into Carol's vision of the wild and inclement Shetland Islands. No matter where the island or what the climate, the colorway speaks to us of untamed beauty and a natural power greater than ourselves.

Learning through Swatching

Although I knit a series of swatches to showcase alternate yarns in most of the projects, no swatch is more important than the gauge or "test" swatch. A typical swatch contains between one and three horizontal and vertical repeats. For the purposes of this exercise, the following swatches for Ocean Moods were knit on US size 2 (2.75 mm) needles, which is the needle size used in the pattern.

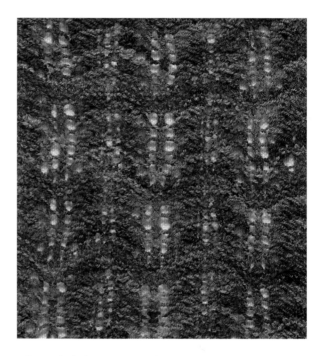

Swatch 1: Lace-Weight Merino in Potluck Colorway

The swatch shown above is an example of a two-ply merino, lace-weight yarn in a Potluck colorway. Merino Lace takes color brilliantly and looks best after blocking. The moderately tight twist produces clean lines that provide excellent pattern and stitch definition while affording just a small amount of stretch. Wool is not as easy to handle as silk because of the stretch, but it does produce beautiful results.

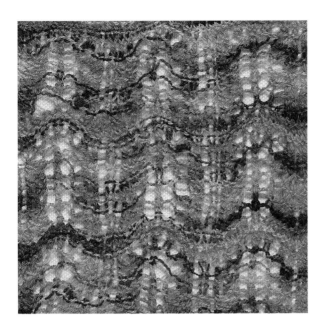

Swatch 2: Lace-Weight Merino in Ocean Colorway

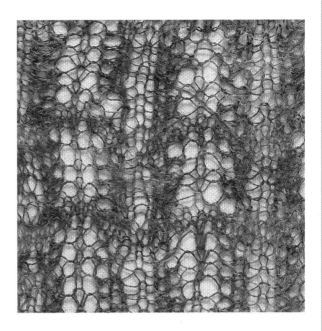

Swatch 3: Suri Lace in Tropical Storm Colorway

This swatch is an example of a lace-weight merino developed and hand painted by Margaret Stove of New Zealand. She calls it Artisan Lace, and the colorway is Ocean. This is a very fine lace yarn designed for very small needles. The colorway proved to be too muted for the ocean mood I was trying to evoke, although it works well in Margaret's own lace scarf designs, which require a strict adherence to a space-dyed color repeat. Here, on my swatch, it looks striped and distracts from the stitch motif. Margaret, however, plays the striped look to its best advantage to produce an ikat effect in her designs. The yarn is too processed and flat for our more free-form approach.

This swatch shows Tropical Storm, the same colorway I chose for Ocean Moods, in a rare luxury fiber called Suri Lace for a totally different look. Suri Lace is a delicate yarn spun from a rare fiber that originates from Peru. Only 6% of the world's alpacas are Suris, a small percentage compared with the more common Huacaya breed from which most alpaca yarn is milled. Suri Lace fiber is considered exotic because of its scarcity. The Suri Lace staple is much longer, finer, and has a distinctive crimp. Common alpaca fiber takes color in a more muted way than wool or silk, and Suri Lace is no different. The inherent fuzziness of the two-ply yarn results in additional softness, which also presents a more muted colorway. On my test needles, it produced a high stretch and works wonderfully for knitting subtle, airy cobweb lace with nap. Like many exotics, Suri Lace is a delicate yarn to handle because of low twist, and it will not withstand much handling without self destructing. Because it is difficult to work with, Suri Lace is not for beginners, but in the hands of an experienced lace maker it produces lace of unparalleled beauty.

Learning Curve

Ocean Moods introduces you to brilliant color in a high-luster yarn that is easy to knit. Never mind that silk is considered a luxury fiber and hand-painted yarn exotic, as both of these factors work to the knitter's advantage. Just remember that the pattern repeat is simple both horizontally and vertically, requiring only garter stitch and simple stitch manipulations. The pattern is brief and easy to memorize, and the ends are self-scalloping, which translates to self-finishing after blocking. Knitters can easily expand this scarf into a larger project by increasing the number of horizontal and vertical repeats to obtain the length and width they prefer.

Technical Tips

Lace patterns can have specific beginning- and end-row layouts that may differ somewhat from the actual repeat. In the chart for Ocean Moods, it is important to put markers between all horizontal repeats and at the inner edges of the repeat. To avoid getting lost or losing count, use a row counter. Rather than put the row counter on a needle, which can cause lack of balance in tension, I wear it on a string around my neck. Often I wear two together, one for horizontal rows and one for vertical repeats. For best results overall, I recommend 10" single-point needles in bamboo or plastic. These materials provide more grip for yarn overs than metal, and more flexibility than wood. It is also important to hold the needles loosely with a quiet hand and wrist, while maintaining moderate tension.

Beginner's Edge

This scarf features easy garter-stitch rows on all four sides. Remember that one garter stitch in width equals two rows of garter stitch in length no matter what yarn you are using. When casting on for the scarf, use the long-tailed cast-on method and cast on very loosely. Slip the first stitch of every row purwise (see page 7). Always

begin the pattern on the right side, which will be the odd-numbered rows. In simple lace such as this, the even-numbered wrong-side rows are knit across, and all patterning takes place on the right-side rows. Bind off the scarf very loosely as well.

If you drop a stitch and can't repair it easily, find it down in the body, anchor it with a safety pin, and repair it with a crochet hook and tie-in thread after blocking is complete. Do not try to repair lace before blocking, and if at all possible, do not rip out knitted rows because many lace yarns are too fragile to withstand repeated ripping and reknitting. If you must "unknit," pick out each stitch individually while keeping all stitches on the needles.

Finished Measurements

Approx 11½" wide by 48½" long after blocking

Materials

1 hank of Cherry Tree Hill Inc. Cascade Fingering
   Silk (100% silk; 150 g, 666 yds per hank) in
   colorway Tropical Storm

Size US 2 (2.75 mm) needles or size to obtain
   gauge

Blocking T pins

Stitch markers

Gauge

Approx 8 sts and 6 rows = 1" in pattern after
blocking

Directions

Sl the first st of every row purlwise; count this st
as one of the garter edge sts.

❖ CO 91 sts and work 2 rows of garter st.

❖ Beg horizontal patt layout on next RS row as
follows: Work 2 sts in garter, PM, referring to
chart, work 14 beg sts, PM, work 12-st patt
rep 5 times (PM between each patt rep), PM,
work 13 end sts, PM, end with 2 sts in garter.

❖ Work 16-row vertical rep a total of 18 times,
ending last vertical rep with completed row
16. Work 2 rows of garter st. BO very loosely.

Blocking

Soak the scarf overnight in cold water without
soap. The next morning, roll it in a towel to press
out excess moisture. Block the scarf immediately
on a flat surface, such as a carpet, bed, blocking
board, or any surface that your pins will anchor
into. Use T pins at scallops on ends and every ½"
to 1" along all sides of the scarf. Start with the ends
and then pin the sides out to the finished measurements in the pattern. You will need to stretch the
garment taut—don't worry, the scarf will not come
apart! Hint: angle pins away from sides to maintain stretch. It will take one to two days to thoroughly dry and only then should you remove the
pins. The scarf will seem stiff, and you will need to
roll it gently in your hands to soften it. A garment
that has been worn many times may need to be
reblocked; this will also restore the shine.

Crest o' the Wave Pattern
12-st horizontal rep
16-row vertical rep

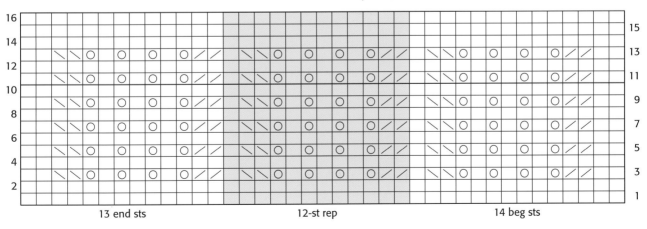

☐ K on both sides	◢ K2tog
⊡ YO	◣ SSK

Irish Mists, Peat Bogs, and Gorse

Designing the Project

BY CAROL RASMUSSEN NOBLE

PICTURE WITH ME the Wicklow Hills of Ireland on an early spring morning: dark, brooding peat bogs; yellow gorse in bloom on the hillsides; a pervasive periwinkle mist.

To express the vision for this project, I chose first a yarn, then a pattern, then a color. I wanted to do a piece in worsted-weight, brushed mohair, a hairy yarn meant to be knit up on large needles. To carry this yarn in lace, I chose an extremely simple Shetland pattern called Razor Shell, which alternates simple open and closed vertical stripes.

For mohair, you need a really simple lace pattern or the effect will be lost in the fuzziness. However, I wanted to include an extra textural element to distinguish the stripe units, so I used a stockinette stitch at the ridge of each herringbone for balance. Of course, this makes Irish Mists a nonreversible piece because, with the addition of stockinette, the two sides are not identical as they would be if done in garter stitch. This is a directional piece of the simplest sort, meaning it is knit from one end to the other, and it is self-scalloping. The yarn presents no tension problems or worries for the beginning knitter and is not intimidating. Beginning lace knitters will love this scarf because there is virtually no finishing. Another advantage is that the scarf requires very little yarn, and the use of large needles ensures that it can be finished quickly.

The colorway is called African Gray, a long way from Irish Mists, but when I put this colorway of Cheryl's together with the pattern and yarn, my personal picture emerged fully detailed. The colors are the colors I saw in my vision, and the hairiness of the yarn blurs over the pattern like a mist. The suggestion of hills in the striping of the color occurred by chance, but enhanced what I wanted to do with this piece.

DESIGNING THE AFRICAN GRAY COLORWAY

BY CHERYL POTTER

The image of shrouded mist reminded me of subtly overdyed yarn. I tried various color combinations in several Potluck batches and was not satisfied because the subtle periwinkle became lost in the dye bath. The colorway finally revealed itself to me as a vision of an African gray parrot—soft, subtle gray and lavender with bright feathers of gold and orange around the eyes. To emphasize the misty hues, I space dyed the colors, interspersing the periwinkle between a silvery gray and shaded purple. The resultant colorway looks at first startling, and yet it works on several levels when knit. Because it is a bold, high-contrast colorway, African Gray is not easily overwhelmed by the mohair yarn. The blazes of bright color allow a vertical orientation not typical of lace knitting, but somehow appropriate here.

The inspiration for African Gray is continents away from the image that inspired Irish Mists, but when we combined the pattern and the yarn, our individual visions merged into a fully realized project.

Learning through Swatching

Super Sport Merino in African Gray Colorway

This swatch is an example of a two-ply, sport-weight yarn in Superwash merino, called Super Sport Merino, and is shown in African Gray, the same colorway as the project scarf. This washable wool has a tight twist that affords it a smooth surface, an even diameter, and durability. Like most Superwash yarns, the fiber takes the color deeply but with a harsh edginess—perfect for socks, but not desirable for lace knitting. The swatch is knit in the same pattern motif with the same needle size as the scarf, and the result is unremarkable at best. Without the textural interest of the mohair, the pattern is much too open and plain. The Razor Shell works best in textured yarns and yarns with high nap. Razor Shell can also be combined with a very stripy yarn, such as dip-dyed or machine-printed yarn, because the motif has such a strong vertical orientation.

Learning Curve

This project introduces you to a lace pattern knit with a very different type of yarn from the first project. By using a nontraditional, worsted-weight, brushed mohair, my goal is to dispel the myth that lace knitting must be done in very fine yarn. As shown here, knitting lace does not necessarily involve plain, thin yarns; small needles; or quiet colors. Thick, fuzzy yarns knit on large needles can be just as successful as "lace" yarns, especially when knit in a riotous colorway as Irish

Mists was. With this project, I hope that new lace knitters will begin to feel comfortable looking outside standard lace yarns for ideas. As your knitting progresses, it will become easier to learn what type of lace is suitable for fuzzy or other nontraditional yarns and how to choose a suitable pattern for a future project of your own outside the scope of this book.

Irish Mists is a good beginner piece because it uses a yarn not typically selected for lace, but has a lace pattern that suits it well. The yarn is easy to handle because it does not stretch or disintegrate, as is the tendency with some fuzzy yarns. The yarn is perfect for the dramatic, sculptural effect of this project. The heavy mohair and high-contrast colorway create and hold interest as the pattern emerges, row after row.

Technical Tips

In the chart for Irish Mists, you will notice that the edge stitch is a single stitch followed by a yarn over. Because the yarn over creates a lace hole, you do not want to slip the first stitch of every row as is usual in lace knitting. Instead, work the first stitch of each row in the pattern. Because this scarf requires no blocking and has virtually no stretch, it requires a tight, nonstretchy edge. For best results, work at moderate tension, avoiding both loopiness and pinching in the knitted fabric. Remember that you can easily modify the size of the project by changing the number of horizontal repeats. Since the vertical repeat is only two rows, it is not necessary to count them. Instead, simply knit until the project is the desired length and end with row three.

Beginner's Edge

In this project, I chose to use a single stockinette stitch on the rib of each herringbone to add loft and to vary surface texture. This enhances the strong verticality of the pattern, which is accentuated by the high-contrast colorway. The pattern features a mixed stockinette and garter ground,

which means that all right-side rows are knit, but all wrong-side rows have both knit and purl stitches. As a result, the scarf will not be identical on both sides. This project demonstrates how some patterns, especially the very simple ones, benefit from textural variation. Design elements of strong color; large-scale, hairy yarn; and a starkly simple stitch pattern combine to produce a harmonious whole. This is the first in a series of lessons that I hope will encourage you to combine whatever elements you choose for your own design in a similarly successful mix. Don't be afraid to break the rules, because in fact, there are no rules, only variables.

Finished Measurements

Approx 10" wide by 46" long

Materials

1 hank of Cherry Tree Hill Inc. Brushed Mohair
(87% mohair, 13% wool; 8 oz, 400 yds per
hank) in colorway African Gray

Size US 9 (5.5 mm) needles or size to obtain
gauge

Stitch markers

Gauge

Approx 4.25 sts and 4 rows = 1" in pattern

Directions

Do not sl the first st of every row.

✤ CO 43 sts and beg patt and follow chart. PM
between patt reps.

✤ Don't bother to count vertical reps. Alternate
rows 2 and 3 until the scarf reaches the
desired length, ending with completed row 3.
Remember that there is no stretch so BO
loosely.

Blocking

Caution: Do not block.

Unlike most lace projects, Irish Mists requires
no blocking. None of any kind should be
attempted, as heat and water will flatten and felt
the hair on the surface of the scarf. Because
mohair is not a stretchy fiber, it cannot be pinned
to better display a lace motif.

Razor Shell Pattern
6-st horizontal rep + 1 st
2-row vertical rep (rows 2 and 3 only)

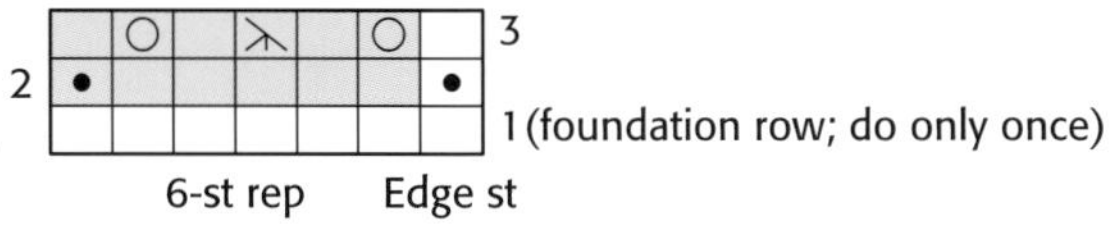

| | O | ⋏ | O | | | 3 |
| 2 | • | | | | • | | 1 (foundation row; do only once) |

6-st rep   Edge st

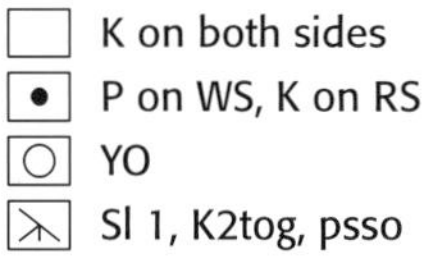

☐ K on both sides
[•] P on WS, K on RS
[O] YO
[⋏] Sl 1, K2tog, psso

A World Lit Only by Fire

Designing the Project

BY CAROL RASMUSSEN NOBLE

I HAVE LONG BEEN A STUDENT of the Middle Ages, and I borrowed this title from a book on the subject that I came across while working on my PhD in Medieval English Literature. This title made me see firelight in darkness, a vision of a room lit only by torches or, even more vivid, a room lit only by candlelight—soft, warm, and glowing fire tones in surrounding darkness.

The lace design I selected to complement my firelight vision of a medieval world is the Shetland Candlelight pattern, which is characterized by a diamond grid. The grid allows the colors to swirl up the diagonals and flicker among the holes like small flames. Cheryl's colorway Cabin Fever was a perfect match to my vision. Although the design appears complex, this pattern is only marginally more difficult to knit than the simpler Crest o' the Wave and Razor Shell patterns found in the first two projects.

The yarn I chose is Merino Superwash DK, a standard yarn that is very nice for general knitting and suited to a pattern with a large motif. I chose this yarn to show that lace can be quite effective and nice in a medium-weight, smooth yarn knit on medium-size needles, and in this way unintimidating—but still lace. It is a project that requires a small amount of yarn and knits up very quickly into a highly wearable piece.

You already know that lace knitting involves manipulating stitches in a repeat to create lace holes. In this pattern, the knitter must not only manipulate more stitches, but also follow diagonal lines in the knitted fabric to create the candle motifs. Remember that you are working with a stockinette stitch ground, rather than garter, which means that there is always a knit side and a purl side.

DESIGNING THE CABIN FEVER COLORWAY

BY CHERYL POTTER

Cabin Fever is a color sequence born of the frustration that I experienced near the end of one long, cold winter in Vermont. I recall the feeling of being confined to my farmhouse, trapped by the freezing weather and swirling snow outside. Stricken by a malaise commonly known as cabin fever, I was sick of the cold gray days that piled one atop the other, and I craved warm weather and the new colors of spring. I knew how it felt to stare feverishly into the too-warm fire, a literal form of cabin fever: sitting mesmerized before the fireplace, watching the orange and red flames lick blackening logs as the swirl of gray smoke disappeared up the chimney. Whether you sit before the fire in a 13th-century castle or hundred-year-old farmhouse, the fireside colors that suggest cabin fever are the same.

Learning through Swatching

I chose to swatch the Candlelight pattern in the same Cabin Fever colorway, but with two other yarns, to show you how to achieve dramatically different results by changing just one element, in this case, the fiber.

Swatch 1: Silk and Merino Worsted in Cabin Fever Colorway

The first swatch is knit in a heavier yarn: a soft, lustrous single-ply, 50% silk/50% merino blend called Silk and Merino Worsted. Here, the colors flow more easily and do not have the harsh edginess of Superwash yarns. Although the colorway is muted, it also has much more depth. Knit into a scarf, the silk-and-merino yarn provides a heavier, more luxurious piece. It looks wonderful in the stockinette ground, but would produce terrible results with a garter ground because a garter ground works best with a very fine yarn and small detailed pattern. The stockinette ground works well with thicker yarns and larger patterns because it shows the shapes more clearly.

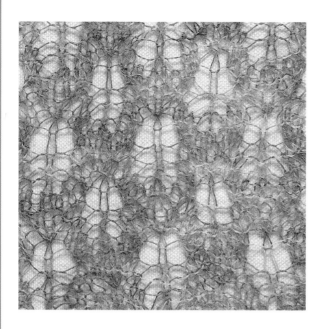

Swatch 2: Suri Lace in Cabin Fever Colorway

In this swatch, which shows the Candlelight pattern knit in a very fine, lace-weight alpaca called Suri Lace, the opposite effect is achieved. With this muted, slightly fuzzy yarn, the pattern motif shows up beautifully in a garter ground and looks thin and uninteresting in a stockinette ground. This occurs because fine yarn looks fuller and can handle more small detail in a garter ground than the Superwash, whereas the Superwash is perfect for larger, bolder effects. I hope, with hands-on practice and using the projects here as a guide, you can begin to understand how knitting "feels" in the two grounds and how to choose the right combinations for your own project.

Learning Curve

In the previous project, Irish Mists, we explored knitting lace with a mixed stockinette and garter ground. A World Lit Only by Fire introduces you to the next level in lace knitting. Candlelight is a pattern that can be knit effectively with either a garter ground or a stockinette ground, but there are elements to consider with either choice. In Superwash Merino DK, the pattern isn't obvious in a garter ground. It takes a stockinette ground with a yarn of this weight to achieve a visual representation of the pattern that works. I encourage knitters to make informed lace choices, in this case, deciding whether a certain yarn looks best with a stockinette ground or garter ground. As in any knitting, the exciting part is that it involves personal choice, whether it be color, texture, fiber, or pattern stitch. Lace knitting can be just as creative as any other type of knitting, especially when working with a painted yarn.

Technical Tips

Tension is very important when alternating knit and purl rows in lace. You will probably find that you need to hold the yarn tighter on the purl side to get an even surface. To achieve an even, stretchy lace edge, remember to slip the first stitch of every row purlwise (with yarn in front). Because this scarf has garter-stitch borders on both edges, on the reverse side you will be knitting four stitches, purling across the pattern section, and then knitting four stitches to complete the garter edge. Try to pull up the yarn a little at the joins of the edges so it does not produce a line of loose gaps. It will help to place a marker between the border stitches and the beginning of the pattern to remind you of the stitch change on the reverse side. On the front, you will be knitting all the way across. Try to keep even tension on your yarn overs as they form diagonals, so that the lace holes are all the same size. This yarn is stretchier than the yarns in the first two projects, hence the need to pay closer attention to your tension.

Beginner's Edge

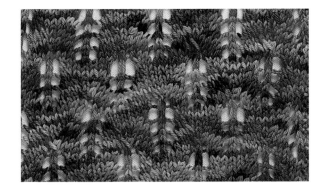

Front

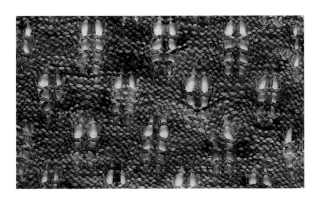

Back

The Candlelight scarf is not reversible; there is a definite right and wrong side to this scarf because of the purl rows on the reverse side.

This slightly more ambitious scarf gives the lace knitter the opportunity to work with a larger motif and a medium-weight yarn. I cannot stress enough the importance of swatching so that you can see the result you will achieve in a larger piece. Swatching allows the lace knitter to explore a variety of alternatives, and this helps the knitter to develop a personal sense of what looks good in lace. As in most knitting, there are no wrong answers, just better choices.

Candlelight is a directional pattern, which means that it is knit from end to end, and that the ends will look different. For this reason, the garter borders are imperative. In a later project requiring more skill, knitters learn a provisional center cast on, which allows the ends to mirror each other.

Finished Measurements

Approx 9" wide by 50" long after blocking

Materials

1 hank of Cherry Tree Hill Inc. Superwash Merino DK (100% washable merino wool; 4 oz, 280 yds per hank) in colorway Cabin Fever

Size US 5 (3.75 mm) needles or size to obtain gauge

Stitch markers

Blocking T pins

Gauge

Approx 5 sts and 5¼ rows =1" in pattern after blocking

Directions

Sl the first st of every row purlwise; count this st as one of the garter edge sts.

✢ CO 49 sts and work 4 rows of garter st.

✢ Beg horizontal patt layout on next RS row as follows: Work 4 sts of garter, PM, referring to chart, work 10 beg sts, PM, 10-st patt rep twice (PM between each patt rep), 11 end sts, PM, end with 4 sts of garter. This layout will give you the equivalent of 4 patt reps plus both sets of garter-st edges. Lace patterns have discrete beginnings and endings, both to create a piece with two finished sides and to preserve the stitch count and pattern continuity.

✢ Work 16-row vertical rep a total of 16 times. Work 4 rows of garter st. BO loosely.

Blocking

Soak the scarf overnight in cold water without soap. The next morning, roll it in a towel and squeeze out excess moisture. Pin the piece out on a flat surface with just enough tension so pattern lies flat. At the same time, it is important to keep the garter edges even.

Candlelight Pattern
10-st horizontal rep
16-row vertical rep

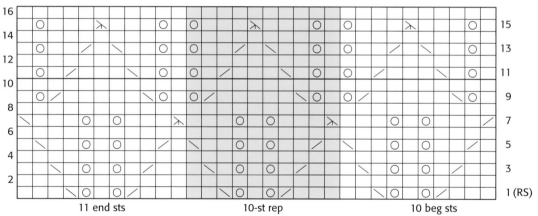

11 end sts   10-st rep   10 beg sts

	K on RS, P on WS
O	YO
⋏	Sl 1, K2tog, psso
╱	K2tog
╲	SSK

La Waytacha

Designing the Project

BY CAROL RASMUSSEN NOBLE

THERE IS A LOVELY CHILDREN'S STORY in Peru about a small girl named La Waytacha ("beloved and respected flower" is a loose translation of the Quechua). She and her very poor family decide to move away from their chacra (small farm) high in the Andes to seek a better life in the big city. All they have fits in her and her mother's carrying blankets. They walk to the city many hundreds of miles away. When they arrive, they are greeted by their citified relatives, but disaster befalls them: they are robbed of almost everything on a city bus. The city people make fun of their traditional dress, and there is no work or shelter for a poor, illiterate rural family. But during all their times of trouble, La Waytacha has a secret that keeps her spirits up.

When she thinks no one is looking, she peeks into her carrying blanket at the treasure she brought from home. One day, her parents notice her behavior and demand that she show them what she is hiding. It is a pot of gold! And with it they have the money to take a bus back to their little village in the high Andes, where they desperately want to return. La Waytacha is a hero. So the family returns with many plans of how to expand their chacra and herds with the gold that is left over. But there is a surprise in store for them. When they get back to their little one-room adobe hut and open La Waytacha's blanket, all that remains is earth that came from their very own fields.

I chose to complete this vision with a Shetland lace design called Checkered Acre, a simple pattern that represents farm fields. To freshen this age-old pattern for the modern lace knitter,

I introduced a new concept I call Crinkle Lace. Here, the surface of the scarf is textured into furrows and ridges created by the yarn overs that all but disappear into this soft, high-nap yarn. The result is a crinkly texture achieved by barely blocking the completed garment, which is knit to its finished size based on gauge before blocking, considered a "mistake" in traditional lace. As an introduction to triangles, the barely blocked square is designed to be folded on the diagonal and worn about the neck like a high Andean cloud.

DESIGNING THE JAVA COLORWAY

BY CHERYL POTTER

Carol recalled the La Waytacha story when she saw a new alpaca yarn I had milled in Peru. The fact that both the yarn and the story originated in the same country proved to be serendipitous, as both designer and colorist gravitated toward Java, a colorway of rich soil and earth tones. To Carol, the shaded browns and grays highlighted by the gold glitter evoked the soil and rock of the Andes with a hint of a dreamscape world in which a pot of gold was possible. For me, the colorway meant the dark hues of the multicolored beans of rich Peruvian coffee hand-picked in the same Andes of Carol's story. The yarn I found for this project is called Glitter Alpaca, a 99% alpaca/1% glitter fingering-weight combination that proved perfect for several reasons. In general, alpaca yarn has a fuzzy quality that also provides drape, especially in the fingering-weight fiber. The Java colorway has hints of gold highlighted by the single strand of gold glitter in the yarn. Because the glitter is only 1%, it adds a subtle spark that is never overbearing and recalls the mystical pot of gold in the Andean fable, making this colorway and yarn a natural choice for the project.

Learning through Swatching

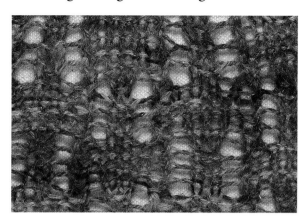

This swatch of the Checkered Acre pattern suffers from over-blocking.

When blocked lightly, the Checkered Acre pattern shows textural interest.

The lesson here is how to determine whether to block heavily or lightly. Not blocking swatches is unheard of, especially in traditional lace knitting where stitch motifs must be washed and pinned and stretched until it seems surely they must break. At the top of the page is an example of the Checkered Acre pattern, knit with the same yarn as the project scarf and heavily blocked as traditional lace. Clearly, it loses all character when stretched, and the motif looks like nothing more than random holes. The simple pattern becomes lost in the lofty alpaca fiber, which in turn loses its beauty when stretched taut.

Compare the blocked swatch to the lightly blocked project garment, and you can see that barely blocking can in some cases add textural interest to a smooth yarn with high nap like Glitter Alpaca.

Learning Curve

What I hope lace knitters are beginning to learn is that even in lace, rules are made to be broken. By now, you must realize that Cheryl and I are leading you down the path of creativity with lace, where after you learn how to get the most out of both yarn and colorway, personal preference will become the only rule not to break. As you progress, it will become second nature to consider the character of a yarn, see the colorway, feel the texture, begin to pull together a complementary pattern, and utilize your sharpened technique to achieve a successful garment. As seen in La Waytacha, even a simple garter ground and stitch motif can combine with exotic yarn and unconventional finishing to create a wonderful, luxurious garment.

Technical Tips

Although most lace benefits from medium to light tension, this project requires tighter tension to produce the crinkle effect. Because the yarn overs should be distinct from the garter stitch, the garter ground needs to be fairly tight. The alpaca is softer and heavier than most lace yarns and tends to knit up loosely, so be certain to hold the yarn with enough firmness to define the stitches. In addition, it is important to minimize stretch in the finished product in favor of drape, and this can only be achieved by monitoring tension.

For these reasons, I recommend avoiding circular and even longish straight needles, because the growing weight stretches the knitting unnecessarily. Single-point Bryspun 10" needles were used on this project. If, upon examining a swatch, you find that you are knitting too loosely to suit your taste, go down two needle sizes. It is also helpful to pull tightly on edge stitches to produce a firm slip stitch, which can tend to get loopy if unattended.

Beginner's Edge

Swatching is especially important for nontraditional lace yarns, because each fiber will behave differently. Because this piece is a square, knitters need to keep track of repeats even though they are simple. Don't forget that the knitted piece must match the finished dimensions before blocking. Here, you do not have the luxury of blocking out slight irregularities. Crinkle Lace requires a soft yarn and a pattern of holes to produce a novel textural surface. It may not look anything like a traditional piece, but don't worry, it is still lace knitting!

When is a square not a square? When you fold it along the diagonal to make a triangle. One of the delightful aspects of this garment is that the square design can be worn as a traditional triangular scarf. Now that we have introduced you to this shape, soon it is time to try some knitted lace triangular scarves and shawls.

Finished Measurements

36" by 36" *before* blocking

Materials

4 skeins of Cherry Tree Hill Inc. Glitter Alpaca
(99% alpaca, 1% glitter; 50 g, 214 yds per
skein) in colorway Java

Size US 4 (3.5 mm) needles or size to obtain
gauge

Stitch markers

Blocking T pins

Gauge

Approx 5 sts and 8 rows = 1" in pattern before
blocking

Directions

Sl the first st of every row purlwise; count this st
as one of the garter edge sts.

✢ CO 176 stitches and work 8 rows of garter st.

✢ Beg horizontal patt layout on next RS row as
follows: Work 2 sts of garter, PM, referring to
chart, work 11 beg sts, PM, work 10-st patt
rep 15 times (PM between each patt rep),
PM, work 11 end sts, PM, end with 2 sts of
garter.

✢ Work 16-row vertical rep a total of 17 times.
Work 8 rows of garter st. BO very loosely.

Blocking

Not all swatches should be blocked the same way,
and this project focuses on the importance of
experimenting with different methods of blocking. While it is dry, pin the square to finished
dimensions on a flat surface without stretching
fabric. With a spray bottle, mist water over garment, enough to wet both sides. Let dry. Unpin
and weave in ends.

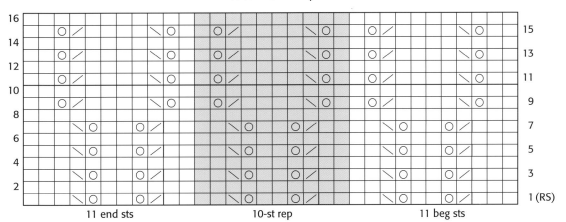

Crinkle Lace (Chequered Acre Pattern)
10-st horizontal rep
16-row vertical rep

☐	K on both sides
○	YO
╱	K2tog
╲	SSK

Sangría

Designing the Project

BY CAROL RASMUSSEN NOBLE

IMAGINE A whitewashed adobe and brick patio with an old wooden table under the sun and shadow of a glittering Spanish afternoon. On the table sits a pitcher of fruited wine, and the sun glints through it in a complex array of reds and golds. It is this picture that came to my mind when I thought of asking Cheryl for Potluck Reds, and Cheryl's dyeing skills produced the perfect mix of color and shade.

The pattern I chose for this piece had to be open and airy to contrast with the density of the colors, so I chose an Icelandic version of Blackberry Stitch done in a lace format, which, for want of a translation, I call Icelandic Bead Stitch Variation because of the way it looks.

This project is our first full-size shawl in a traditional triangular design. Although it is larger than our previous projects, the bigger needles and easy pattern stitch ensure a quick knit, even for novice lace knitters.

The yarn Cheryl found for me is a baby mohair bouclé. Mohair comes from the Angora goat, and this yarn is a blend of mostly mohair bouclé with a touch of wool spun around a nylon core, which stabilizes the more fragile mohair. This lofty loop yarn not only takes color beautifully, but is also perfect for the open-and-closed nature of the pattern motif.

DESIGNING THE POTLUCK REDS COLORWAY

BY CHERYL POTTER

One of the characteristics of Potluck yarns is that, unlike traditional hand-painted yarns, there is no visible repeat in the color sequence. In a similar colorway like Cabin Fever, for example, the red always follows the peach and in turn segues into black. In a Potluck, reds can be placed next to peach in one section and then several colors away from peach somewhere else, for example, or never seen again. In this way, colors are allowed to build upon one another, and deep overdyes of complex shades result, much like sun penetrating rich red wine.

differences between the swatches, keep in mind that Potluck, even if it were the same color combination—an impossible task—would look different in animal and plant fibers. Cottons tend to mute dye, and they do not spread color as readily as animal fibers do. North Country Cotton offers the added complication of a matte finish, which does nothing to move the color along, unlike the bouclé in the project shawl. Although the yarn takes the dye in a bright, contrasting way, it has no highlights. The stitch definition is sharp, yet the smoothness of the yarn contributes to a textural void that makes for a dull, pedestrian shawl.

Learning through Swatching

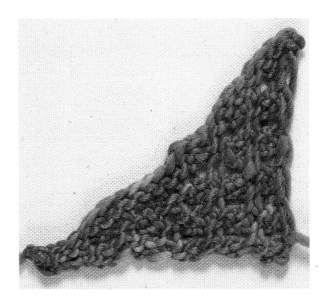

Swatch 2: Lamb's Pride Worsted in Potluck Colorway

Swatch 1: North Country Cotton
in Potluck Reds Colorway

The first swatch shows a 100% mercerized cotton yarn called North Country Cotton, knit on the same size needles as the Sangría shawl. This is a much heavier worsted-weight yarn, and it is also shown in Potluck Reds. As you notice the startling

The second swatch shows Lamb's Pride Worsted, an 85% wool/15% mohair blend also knit in a Potluck combination of reds. This worsted-weight animal-fiber yarn takes the dye in a much more interesting way: the single ply allows the dye to travel easily and the mohair provides shine. Although Potluck yarn can look splotchy on the skein, it has highlights that can be shown to their best advantage with the right pattern stitch. Hand-painted Lamb's Pride is not the right yarn for the project, as it is simply too thick to produce a pleasant and beautiful shawl. Although the stitch definition is evident, the pattern and color combination cries out for fine yarn with texture.

Learning Curve

This garment introduces several new ideas at once. It is the first triangular design I offer but is not difficult to knit as long as you count carefully. It is also the first garment knit with Potluck color and involving yarn texture as a design consideration. We both invite the designer that dwells within you to begin to reflect on the interplay of these elements. As your knowledge of lace expands, it will become easier to incorporate color, texture, and pattern into a cohesive design. In the project garment, the triangle is the shape that melds color and texture into a unique piece. The Potluck, essentially a one-of-a-kind yarn, allows absolute freedom within the structural triangle. The texture both breaks up the color and moves it along, so that no complicated pattern stitch is needed.

Technical Tips

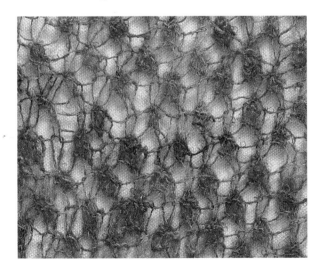

The open and airy pattern pattern works well with Baby Loop Mohair.

Counting is important in this piece because a single stitch on a first right-side row becomes three stitches on the next right-side row and vice versa.

The increases are achieved by knitting yarn overs at the beginning of each row. Therefore, it is not necessary to slip the first stitch purlwise, because the first stitch is always a yarn over. Be careful not to lose the yarn overs! Work out your own system of placing markers if necessary.

I recommend placing markers between every four-stitch unit, which would be eight stitches total. I would also place markers on each side of the central stitch unit because the shawl is designed to have a center-back column. As each end of the needle accrues enough stitches to create another four-stitch unit, place a marker on the needle. Don't worry about the number of markers you use; they come off easily.

It also helps to differentiate the right side from the wrong side at the outset, for though both sides look the same, they are knit differently. Patterning is done on the right side, and garter stitch on the wrong side, but the first stitch must be a new yarn over on each side. Knit with extremely loose tension to allow the stitches to fill out into beads and to help with the rigorous blocking that this shawl requires.

Beginner's Edge

Because you must knit with loose tension, this project is best suited to metal needles. The stitches need to slide effortlessly. Keep the yarn overs loose, but not so big that you lose them altogether. This shawl is easy to make bigger or smaller. To enlarge it, just keep going. You will find that there is plenty of yarn in the eight-ounce hank. But remember, it is important to purchase all the yarn you need in one batch, because Potluck is unique yarn and cannot be duplicated.

Finished Measurements

(after blocking)

Center back: Approx 40"
Top width: Approx 80"

Materials

1 hank of Cherry Tree Hill Inc. Baby Loop Mohair
(88% mohair, 10% wool, 2% nylon; 8 oz,
1000 yds per hank) in colorway Potluck Reds

Size US 9 (5.5 mm) needles or size to obtain
gauge

2 packets of stitch markers

Blocking T pins

Gauge

Approx 5 sts and 3¼ rows = 1" in pattern after
blocking

Directions

Because the first st of every row is a YO, you will
not sl the first st.

❖ CO 1 st. Beg first row of chart: YO, PM, K1,
K1 tbl, K1, PM. Once you are familiar with 4-
row vertical patt, cont until you have completed 32 vertical patt reps up the center
block. PM as indicated in "Technical Tips."

❖ It is important to BO extremely loosely. The
shawl may at this point look like a bunched-
up rag to you, but your ugly duckling is about
to become a swan.

Blocking

This is the first piece in which we introduce the
traditional notion of heavy blocking. Do not think
you have made a mistake if you find your garment
really needs stretching. This is the nature of fine
lace. To open the yarn overs, it is necessary to pull
the edges when wet. Once dry, the shawl will keep
its shape until the next washing.

Soak shawl overnight in cold water without
soap. Block it soaking wet on a flat surface. Be
aware that it requires rigorous stretching to reach
the blocked dimensions and the finished look.
Don't be afraid to pull on the fabric; the yarn is
very strong.

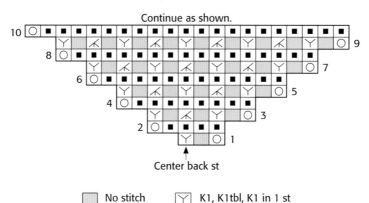

Icelandic Bead St Variation
Start each row with YO.
Internal rep is 4 sts and 4 rows.

Continue as shown.

Center back st

	No stitch		K1, K1tbl, K1 in 1 st
■	K on WS		K3tog
○	YO		

Peacock's Pride

Designing the Project

BY CAROL RASMUSSEN NOBLE

FOR THIS PROJECT I took my first impression from the colorway Peacock, one of my favorites among all of Cheryl's gorgeous colors. When I look at this colorway, I see a stately grouping of peacocks with their tails at full glory, moving across a wide expanse of manicured lawn on a lost summer afternoon.

With the peacock idea in mind, I went looking for a traditional pattern that I thought reflected my vision. I wanted to do something that I call Aran Lace, so my research went in that direction. What I found was an old Aran pattern of opening fans that reminded me of peacocks' tails. Although simple to knit, being only a knit-and-purl base pattern with holes, this pattern has a pleasing textural look

that belies its simplicity. To make more texture, I added a twist stitch interlacement. This part of the pattern was traditionally knit using a cable needle, but I decided to simplify again and got the same effect with a series of twist maneuvers that are easier to manage.

Choosing the yarn was more difficult. I wanted a soft, sturdy yarn without high nap or heaviness, but something that could shine through a textured Aran pattern. I chose Silk and Merino DK, a double knitting-weight blend that is 50% silk and 50% merino, although a worsted-weight yarn would have worked equally well. The addition of the merino gives the yarn some memory and lightness—we were afraid that a 100% silk, single-ply yarn we were considering would stretch and pull the motif out of shape.

DESIGNING THE PEACOCK COLORWAY

BY CHERYL POTTER

Peacock is a standard colorway for me, but one that changes as the dye sets. The greenish gold color, which represents the "eye" of the peacock feather, looks very different on various yarns. I, too, thought of the fantail spread of the peacock feathers and the way the colors move up the feather and around the fan. This is a longish colorway that does not have the repeat that a shorter, simpler colorway would have; the colors are urged to meet and blend, creating secondary colors between. As a result, the shades created on the skein are more exciting than the initial colors applied to the yarn.

Learning through Swatching

Swatch 1: 8-Ply New Zealand Wool in Dusk Colorway

For the first swatch, Cheryl suggested an eight-ply (DK) New Zealand 100% wool shown in the colorway Dusk. I used the same-size yarn, the same pattern motif, and the same-size needle as our project scarf. Notice how the New Zealand wool gives the pattern less shine and a more rugged look.

Dusk is a rich colorway of saturated hues shown in a sunset configuration. The purple and blue combination shadowed by green reminds me of fathomless waves roiling up to crash as

surf. The deep colors are akin to the deep water, and the paler shades are the crests of the waves as they break a curl. Here, the fan pattern stitch becomes the surf spreading on the sand, and the holes are the foam at its margin.

DESIGNING THE DUSK COLORWAY

BY CHERYL POTTER

The fan motif complements the Dusk colorway. Dusk is a sunset colorway, which means that colors advance toward one central shade and then retreat, much as color spreads as the sun sets over the horizon. Here, the blues, purples, and green merge toward a central burgundy and then fade away, much like the pounding of the waves or the waves of color in a fan.

Overall, Dusk works just as well as Peacock when creating a form and function vision for the project scarf. The unique image is just a combination of elements rearranged to create a new story. The lace you knit will develop personal meaning as you create your own story.

Swatch 2: Lamb's Pride Worsted in Potluck Red Colorway

This swatch is shown in a yarn from the previous chapter, used for sampling the motif for the Sangría shawl. It is Lamb's Pride Worsted, an 85% wool and 15% mohair yarn by Brown Sheep, shown in hand-dyed Potluck Red. Like the project yarn, it is a soft, single ply of blended fibers, but slightly thicker, and shows the Aran Lace pattern clearly. The addition of the mohair creates nap. When I examined the color combinations, I envisioned the warm browns, terra cottas, and mauves of a muddy river in the Amazon jungle. None of the jungle rivers are blue; all their tones are the rich earth colors we see in this yarn. As the feeder streams lazily run out from the vegetation and join the larger river, they bring with them a miniature delta where the terra cotta of one stream feathers out like a fan into the brown of another. The fan motif of the pattern echoes this outflow.

DESIGNING THE POTLUCK RED COLORWAY

BY CHERYL POTTER

I had a vision similar to Carol's. I saw the colors as the mud churned up by a Mississippi paddleboat as it chugs from the Gulf of Mexico to New Orleans. Here, the shallow, muddy river widens and flattens out, torn only by the wheel of the paddleboat, as the water fans out behind on a hot and still summer day. The slow spread of water echoes the motif in the design. This vision is yet another recombination of similar but different elements designed to lead the lace knitter-designer farther down the path of creative imagination.

Learning Curve

Typically, I begin a more detailed discussion here of what is to be learned from knitting this piece. But entertain for a moment the possibility of a different governing vision or of multiple visions. I found inspiration for this scarf on the basis of color. But what if the yarn chosen was not painted in a Peacock colorway and so didn't remind you of a peacock? In fact, what if you had come across the Aran motif first, without any knowledge of the colorway? It is important to

find inspiration at whatever point you enter into the design mix and to feel confident about building a cohesive piece of lace from there, as the two previous swatches illustrate.

Technical Tips

To avoid loops, knit this pattern with medium tension and pull up slightly on the yarn when changing from knit stitch to purl stitch. If you pull too tightly, your twists will shrink up, so make sure you are knitting an allover flat surface. There is stretch in this yarn, and it needs blocking. Do not overmanipulate the yarn. It is a single ply, which by its very nature is softer and more delicate than plied yarns, and it has a light twist. You want a soft yarn for a neck scarf, but if the overriding concern is rich texture, consider a plied yarn, such as the New Zealand wool used for the first swatch. The Silk and Merino can pill, so avoid abrading the surface before it is

blocked and handle the wet piece with care.

The twist stitch is practical for small, single cables and works well for socks and gloves as well as lace. Monitor the tension of the twists to make sure they are even. Stitches cannot be too tight or too loose. I suggest swatching

Close-Up of the Twist Stitch

the twist itself with some scrap yarn for practice. Once you see how simple it is, you will find the twist stitch a quick and easy substitute for a cable.

Beginner's Edge

Lace knitters encounter many new factors in this project. As far as technique goes, knitters will discover how to do simple Aran work and a twist stitch, while refining tension skills. Lace knitters will also learn how to handle very soft twist yarn and how to block it. As designers, we both hope you come away with an idea of how to allow yourself to be inspired by yarn, color, or pattern and how to translate this personal vision into coherent knitting.

Finished Measurements

Approx 7" wide by 50" long after blocking

Materials

1 hank Cherry Tree Hill Inc. Silk & Merino DK (50% silk, 50% Merino wool; 4 oz, 313 yds per hank) in colorway Peacock

Size US 5 (3.75 mm) needles or size to obtain gauge

Stitch markers

Gauge

Approx 6.5 sts and 4¾ rows = 1" in pattern after blocking

Directions

Sl the first st of every row purlwise; count this st as one of the garter edge sts.

❖ CO 47 sts and work 2 rows in garter st.

❖ Beg horizontal patt layout on next RS row as follows: Work 4 sts in garter, PM, referring to chart, work 6-st twist cable, PM, work 27-st fan patt, PM, work 6-st twist cable, PM, end with 4 sts in garter.

❖ Work 8-row vertical fan patt rep a total of 30 times. Work 2 rows in garter st. BO loosely.

Blocking

Soak scarf overnight in cold water without soap. Carefully lift the wet piece onto a towel and roll to squeeze out excess moisture. Lay piece on flat surface and pull slightly to reach the finished dimensions. Pinning is neither required nor desirable. Allow scarf to dry thoroughly. Remember that reblocking will restore luster to silk.

Fan Pattern
27-st horizontal pattern including beg and end sts
8-row vertical rep

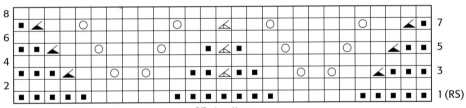

27-st pattern

Twist-Stitch Cable
6-st horizontal pattern
12-row vertical rep

6-st pattern

K on RS, P on WS

P on RS, K on WS

YO

P2tog

P3tog

Knit into back of second st on left needle, do not slip st off needle, knit into first st on left needle, slip both sts off needle.

Knit first 2 sts tog on left needle, do not slip sts off needle, knit into first st on needle, slip both sts off needle.

Note: The row counts and repeats will be different for the two patterns. If you have trouble seeing it, make yourself a chart of corresponding rows and mark off each one. You will soon discover that you can do the repeats of each pattern by sight.

Falling Leaves

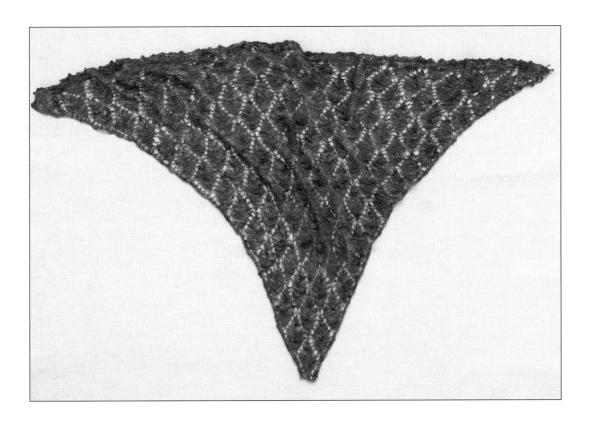

Designing the Project

BY CAROL RASMUSSEN NOBLE

AUTUMN ARRIVES EARLY on the shores of Lake Superior, and I lived several fall seasons there, enjoying the riot of color. The Great Lakes region is heavily forested with stands of pine and deciduous trees. The red leaves of the sugar maples stand out against the lighter mauves and russets of the poplar, birch, and oak leaves. The pines, so dark green as to seem nearly black, punctuate the mix. It is this rich landscape that I recognized in Cheryl's new colorway Foxy Lady, a space-dyed sequence of reds and russets highlighted by mauve, turned fawn and slate.

To further my vision of fall scenery at the edge of the Great Lakes, I chose a Shetland pattern called Falling Leaves to echo the color scheme in shapes. It is a large motif, suitable for a stockinette ground and a showy colorway. As in A World Lit Only by Fire, this pattern is a large, flat, diamond grid. The larger and flatter the motif, the more likely it is to show to its best advantage in the

matte finish texture of stockinette. The center leaf ridge shows up well against the stockinette ground, as do the larger holes. These lace holes provide more contrast to the ground than they would in a finer garter-stitch lace, where texture is not desired and the detail comes from finely packed rows of garter ground and a profusion of small holes. Stockinette patterns like Falling Leaves are a perfect palette for a contrast colorway such as Foxy Lady, which requires a broader brush stroke. The colors twine around the diagonals and leaves in bold relief, obscuring the subtlety possible in a fine garter ground. The large motif and bold colors invite the use of a novelty yarn, because the large areas of solid ground and the longer loops of the yarn overs allow it to exhibit contrasts in texture, color, and luster.

The yarn Cheryl found for me to emphasize the large motif pattern for this triangular shawl is called Ariel, which is a novelty yarn in 65% cotton and 35% rayon. The yarn is a loosely stranded two ply, and the rayon wrapped around the cotton has a small ribbon seed, called a slub, every few inches. These bits of ribbon tend to dye more brilliantly than the two-ply yarn and create an interesting movement of texture and color within the movement of the colorway itself. Not only is this the first pattern in which I use a cotton yarn for lace, it is also the first pattern in which I introduce a novelty yarn. Cotton is no one's first choice for lace, but knitters with wool allergies are turning to it more and more. It is simple to wash and block and not heavy, so that it is versatile for warmer weather and climates.

At first, Ariel may appear to be unsuitable for lace because of its uneven surface. However, it merely requires the right pattern and color format to show it to its best advantage, as in Falling Leaves. Here, knit on larger needles, the color and texture interplay spreads over the entire group of motifs for a look of shimmering beauty. Because Ariel is a slub yarn, it requires a large motif that will not get lost in the textured yarn, as is so often the case with a novelty yarn. Whenever you run color and texture together with a pattern stitch, you need to decide which element gets the most emphasis, and I have chosen to let the texture shine in this case. Although large, the motif is simple, and is set on a plain stockinette ground with a predictable repeat. The colorway stays in the same color family—earth

---

DESIGNING THE FOXY LADY COLORWAY

BY CHERYL POTTER

Foxy Lady is a newer colorway for me, and in it, I experiment with the interplay of light- and dark-contrast earth tones. I purposely spaced bright reds and brick next to watered chocolate to create the sense of frost-touched, faded leaves. The gray is a green-based black, which breaks to greenish slate when stressed. My vision is of a vixen in fall, threading her way through the stark trees and fallen leaves to the safety of her den. In the forest she is a brilliant splash of deep reds and russets, and then she is gone like a ghost.

---

tones—and is also not distracting. It is the yarn itself, with its unpredictable ribbon seeds and stranded loose twist—not to mention the fact that the cotton and rayon take the dye differently—that boosts the texture and elevates this shawl to a piece of wearable art. As in most cases with novelty yarns, we let the yarn do the work. This is not traditional or fine lace, but who said it had to be?

Learning through Swatching

As this is the only cotton shawl in the book, Cheryl suggested swatching the Falling Leaves pattern in the same Foxy Lady colorway, but with two other cottons. Here I explore the nature of cotton lace and how to achieve dramatically different results by changing just one element—in this case, texture.

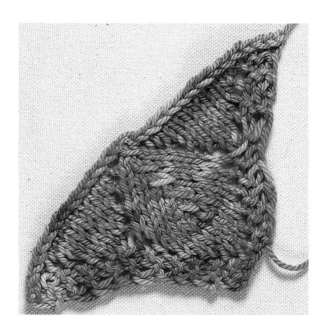

Swatch 1: North Country Cotton
in Foxy Lady Colorway

This swatch is knit in North Country Cotton, a worsted-weight, four-ply, mercerized, smooth cotton. This is a heavier yarn than the one used in the project shawl. Unlike the Ariel, which is a rayon slub yarn spun around a cotton core, this fiber contains no novelty component and has no shine. The pure cotton takes the color in a subdued fashion with an unexciting matte finish. The motif looks bigger because this yarn is thicker and must be knit on larger needles. The resultant garment would look ordinary compared to the whimsical look of the Ariel.

Swatch 2: Cotton Bouclé in Foxy Lady Colorway

In this swatch, knit in a novelty yarn called Cotton Bouclé, the opposite effect is achieved. Although this yarn is even thicker—a heavy, worsted-weight 100% cotton—it offers a subtle texture that lends the colorway an interesting appeal. Like the North Country Cotton, the Cotton Bouclé takes the colorway in a muted way. Because it is bulkier than the Ariel, it knits up quickly on larger needles and provides a quick-knit shawl with some textural variation. The texture is mild and predictable compared to the Ariel, which has a random ribbon slub that can appear anywhere in the knitting. Cotton Bouclé is more suited to sweaters than shawls, but for a quick-knit cotton shawl, it would prove a better choice than the North Country Cotton.

Learning Curve

This novelty shawl is fun to knit and fun to wear. All the versions of Falling Leaves swatched are shawls for those who live in warmer climates or for summer. We both enjoy the silky feel of the Ariel and the highlights offered by the slubby rayon and understand that unlike a traditional shawl, Falling Leaves is not meant for warmth, but show. This garment drapes beautifully and does not lose its shine with handling. Another advantage is that the shawl is a one-hank wonder, meaning that the entire garment can be knit from one hank of Ariel. This not only cuts the cost of knitting the project, but also saves the knitter from the frustration of having to match dye lots or weave in ends from several small hanks.

With Falling Leaves, I expand on the theme of simple triangles that began with the Sangría shawl, which increases by working yarn overs at both edges. This triangular piece also increases by a yarn over at the beginning of each row, but here, the yarn over comes inside the garter stitch border and is part of the stockinette ground. It is important to note that the diamond pattern offers a natural increase along each side as the new motifs are added. In this sense, its growth is organic like the Sangría shawl. It is the easiest increase to use when beginning to design triangular shawls because the pattern is stretched flat across the back from one side to the other and vertically straight up and down.

Technical Tips

Knit this yarn at loose tension because it is not the same diameter overall. Place markers at the insides of the three-stitch garter borders and between motifs, and place additional markers as you knit more motifs. Otherwise, counting all the yarn overs and determining their placement can become problematic. Make sure to slip the first stitch of every row purlwise; these stitches will form the outside border edge, and you will need a very stretchy edge for blocking.

At the beginning of the new motifs that are added along each edge, knitters will actually be starting with a three-stitch increase on the first row: YO (yarn over), M1 (make 1), YO. This will not show in the finished piece as it blocks out normally. Also, it is important to place markers at each side of the new three-stitch-motif section. This may sound confusing, but a glance at the chart should clarify.

Beginner's Edge

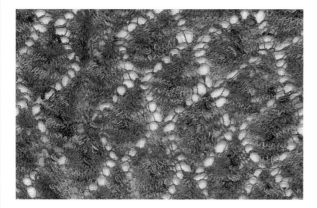

The complex look of the falling leaves design is actually deceptively simple.

This is the most involved pattern motif offered yet, and with the complication of a triangular shape and a novelty yarn, it can look daunting. But when you break down the design, it is actually deceptively simple. As mentioned before, all increases are done as yarn overs just inside the garter edge and do not affect the pattern stitch, and there are no partial motifs to consider. The motif is easier than it looks as well. The right-side rows, which contain the lace pattern, are all knit across. The wrong-side rows will be as follows: K3, purl across pattern area, K3. After you see how the first two rows are knit, the pattern stitch becomes easy. There is no complex math and there are no decreases in pattern along a center rib. This type of triangular shawl design progresses in a rhythmic fashion that is easy to knit and easy to grasp conceptually. It is really a self-explanatory shawl. The addition of a striking colorway and a novelty blend only fuels the excitement of completing this unique garment.

Finished Measurements

(after blocking)

Center back: 40"
Top length: 78"

Materials

1 hank of Cherry Tree Hill Inc. Ariel (65% cotton, 35% rayon; 8 oz, 515 yds per hank) in color-way Foxy Lady

Size US 5 (3.75 mm) needles or size to obtain gauge

2 packages of stitch markers

Blocking T pins

Gauge

Approx 3¾ sts and 3¾ rows = 1" in pattern after blocking

Directions

Sl the first st of every row purlwise; count this st as one of the garter edge sts.

✤ CO 6 sts and beg row 1 of chart as follows: Work 3 sts in garter, YO, end 3 sts in garter. For the remainder of the patt, follow chart as shown, always working the first and last 3 sts of every row in garter st. Notice that the patt itself is worked on a St st ground. PM as discussed in "Technical Tips."

Note: To ease the beginning lace knitter into the rhythm of increases while creating a motif such as Falling Leaves, all increases are done by yarn overs at the beginning and end of each patt row in the places between the 3-stitch garter outline and the stockinette patt. This sounds much more complicated than it really is. Actually what happens is you just keep adding motifs on each side in a natural progression of the diagonal lines of yarn overs. The chart shows one complete vertical and horizontal repeat plus a few extra rows to clarify the increase.

✤ Cont in patt until you have 8 completed leaves in a column up center back. You do not need to count horizontal reps because they come organically from knitting a triangle of diamond patterns. Partial motifs occur only along top row because every other full leaf is sided by half leaves horizontally. To increase size of shawl, just knit more diamonds up center back and allow patt to flow naturally from diagonals.

✤ Work 5 rows in garter st. BO very loosely.

Blocking

Soak shawl overnight in cold water without soap. Block soaking wet on a large, flat surface. The yarn does not run and surprisingly has very little stretch when dry. This garment requires rigorous pulling and high tension while drying to maintain its finished shape. I recommend using plenty of pins for good coverage of the edges. When totally dry, unpin and weave in ends.

Large Leaf Pattern

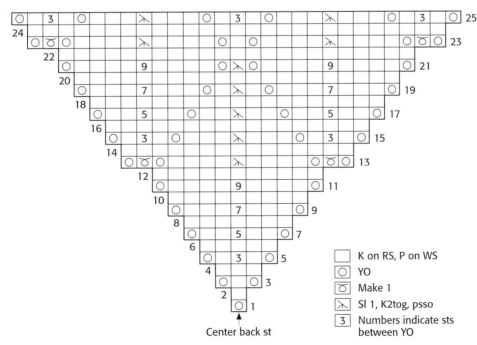

Center back st

	K on RS, P on WS
○	YO
⌒	Make 1
⋋	Sl 1, K2tog, psso
3	Numbers indicate sts between YO

Chancay Morning

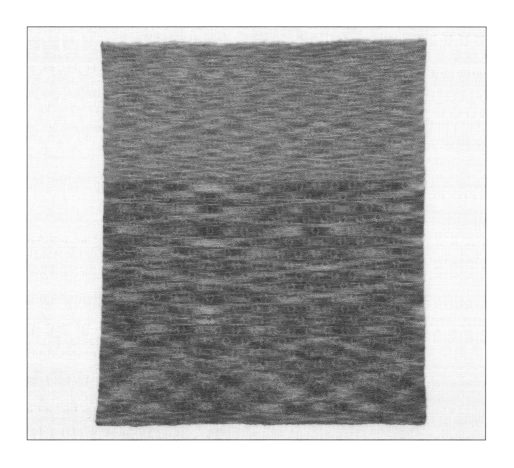

Designing the Project

BY CAROL RASMUSSEN NOBLE

THE PERUVIAN COAST is the driest desert in the world. The desert is narrow, a mere strip between the sea and the Andes, and at some points, the mountains come all the way to the sea in bizarre, moonlike landscapes and precipitous cliffs. These skeletal mountains, devoid of vegetation, are cut through all along the coast by narrow, canyonlike valleys with small rivers irrigating them. In the lengthy pre-Columbian period, each of these isolated valleys gave rise to different cultures at different times. Because of the dryness, many of the artifacts and mummy bundles are well preserved. Some of these cultures, such as the Mochica, made wonderful pots. Others, such as the Paracas and the one we are dealing with here, the Chancay, produced glorious woven textiles. Chancay is an area to the north of Lima with a wider swath of arable land than is typical farther south. The Chancay people buried their textiles with their dead in shallow pits in the desert ground, leading to their almost perfect state of preservation. The colors, all vegetable dyes, are exactly like the colors in Cheryl's colorway Indian Summer—golds, fuchsias, pinks, mauves—colors as rich today in many intact museum pieces as they were when they were made.

By the way, knitting was unknown to these peoples before the Spanish brought it after the Conquest. As you can see, many happy memories of time spent appreciating the county's history while living and traveling in Peru came back to me to produce the inspiration for this vivid daydream shawl.

Many of the tapestry woven motifs of the Chancay were geometric, others zoomorphic. One of the most popular and my personal favorite is the stylized jaguar called "el tigre." That is why I chose, cross-culturally, a Shetland pattern of a stylized cat's paw for these colors. To complete my dreamscape, I chose an Andean fiber, baby alpaca, in a very fine lace-weight yarn with great luster and drape.

Swatch 2: Kid Mohair in Indian Summer Colorway

DESIGNING THE INDIAN SUMMER COLORWAY

BY CHERYL POTTER

Indian Summer is not a sunrise colorway for me, but it is just as fleeting, for its flash-in-the-pan hues herald one last hurrah for summer before New England prepares for winter. Indian summer is a carefree reprieve that can last two weeks in Vermont, but some years doesn't happen at all. I envision Indian paintbrushes in fields of bleached grass at October's end, and stark maples standing in a soft carpet of fallen leaves, silent witnesses to one last brilliant riot of wildflowers.

Learning through Swatching

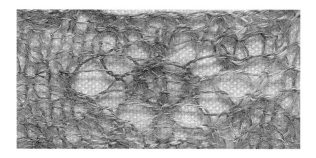

Swatch 1: Suri Lace in Indian Summer Colorway

This swatch is knit in Suri Lace. It has a long, lustrous staple and is shown here as a two-ply lace-weight yarn, which is the same weight and colorway as the project yarn. Since it's knit in the same Cat's Paw pattern as the project, the only remaining variable is fiber content. As this motif requires a fine yarn, you might think the Suri Lace would be appropriate, but it lacks the body to support a scarf such as this one, which requires only light blocking. When knit into such a fine allover texture, Suri Lace becomes so stretchy that it requires rigorous blocking. The yarn proved too lightweight for this project, and although the Baby Alpaca is also considered lace weight, the silk component makes it a heavier fiber with more drape.

This swatch is knit in Kid Mohair, a lace-weight, brushed mohair, also knit with the Indian Summer colorway in the Cat's Paw pattern. Although heavy enough, this yarn does not produce the fine allover surface of the Baby Alpaca yarn. The problem is that such a high-nap fiber as brushed mohair requires knitting on much larger needles. This means that the scale of the square with its fine, finished look becomes unobtainable because the motif is both obscured by the mohair and knit too large. The fuzzy look blurs the yarn overs and makes the motifs difficult to recognize, even though they are knit on bigger needles.

In either Suri Lace or Kid Mohair, both motif and pattern can be modified and used successfully in either of these swatching yarns. The results would be different, not less beautiful, but not in keeping with the original vision. Remember that this is merely my current vision and we both invite you to choose your own.

Learning Curve

This piece is knit as a versatile square that can be worn as a headscarf or folded in half and draped decoratively about the neck. Baby Alpaca is the first actual lace-weight yarn used for a project so far, and care must be taken with gauge and finished measurements, as this is a garment that will be only very lightly blocked. The Cat's Paw pattern area has a garter ground framed by seed-stitch borders. By now, you know that lace yarn does not always have to be "lacy" as seen here. The combination of fine knitting, a small motif, and a subtle colorway produces an understated scarf that is both luxurious and elegant, but not difficult to knit as long as you faithfully count stitches and rows.

Technical Tips

This project is an exercise in hand skills, as the scarf must be knit with tight, even tension. The fact that it is knit in garter stitch rather than stockinette stitch is beneficial, because most knitters have a different tension on knit and purl rows. This is why many designers choose garter stitch for fine knitting with fine yarns; every row—whether right side or wrong side—is a knit row. Cast-on stitches, bound-off stitches, and the first slipped stitch along the edge must be stretchy, but not loopy. Make sure the yarn overs are not too tight, which produces puckering, or too loose, which produces gapping. It is important to create an even, unblocked surface and to think of this as a design feature, especially when knitting squares, which must have the same horizontal and vertical dimensions.

This yarn is delicate and cannot take ripping out. It is time to feel confident with the successful lace knitting accomplished so far and to plan not to unknit rows. Counting is of great importance because of the distance between motifs. Mark each repeat and carefully count unpatterned stitches and rows. A row counter is advisable.

Beginner's Edge

The secret to success with this garment is counting rows and motifs correctly from the beginning so the piece is laid out properly. As mentioned before, the patterning is based upon two staggered stripes of discrete motifs—the first with 17 Cat's Paws and the second with 16—which make up the vertical repeat. You will notice that this lace square is composed of garter stitches in the center and seed stitches along the borders.

Remember that this is your first try with a very fine lace yarn; do not feel daunted by the number of stitches and rows. As long as you knit this pattern with even tension row by row, you are assured of beautiful results: a sophisticated and unique garment of fine lace.

The Cat's Paw pattern is easy to knit if you count stitches and rows carefully.

Finished Measurements

37" by 37" after light blocking

Materials

3 hanks of Cherry Tree Hill Inc. Baby Alpaca (80% baby alpaca, 20% silk; 50 g, 437 yds per hank) in colorway Indian Summer

Size US 2 (2.75 mm) needles or size to obtain gauge

2 packages of stitch markers

Blocking T pins (optional)

Gauge

Approx 8 sts and 15 rows = 1" in pattern after blocking

Directions

Sl the first st of every row purlwise; count this st as one of the seed edge sts.

Seed Stitch

Row 1 (RS): K1, P1 across, end K1.
Row 2 (WS): P1, K1 across, end P1.

✤ CO 293 sts and work 20 rows of seed st.

✤ Beg horizontal patt layout on next RS row as follows: Work 10 seed sts, PM, referring to chart, work 9 beg sts, PM, work 16-st patt rep 16 times (PM between each patt rep), PM, work 8 end sts, PM, end with 10 seed sts.

✤ Work 32-row vertical rep a total of 16 times, then work the first 18 rows of chart once more. Work 20 rows of seed st. BO very loosely.

Blocking

Lay piece out dry on flat surface and shape it to square dimensions. Pins are optional. Using spray bottle, mist entire surface with cold water until both sides are damp. Allow to dry, then weave in ends.

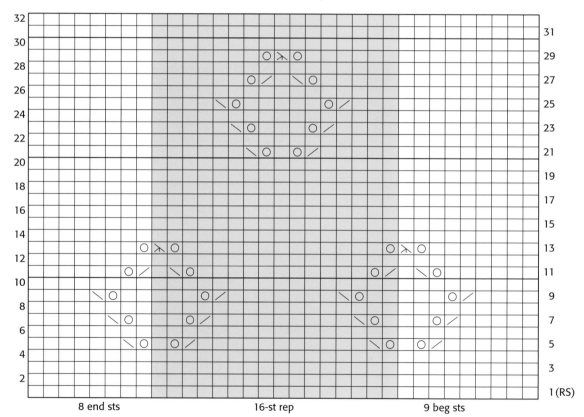

Cat's Paw Variation
16-st horizontal rep
32-row vertical rep

	K on both sides
O	YO
⋏	Sl 1, K2tog, psso
╱	K2tog
╲	SSK

Parrot House

Designing the Project

BY CAROL RASMUSSEN NOBLE

IMAGINE YOURSELF in the Amazon jungle: sinuous, lush, sinister green walls enclose you, brown rivers snake through the vegetation, and striking flashes of color appear as parrots fly up and settle again. This is the world I saw in Cheryl's one-of-a-kind Potluck Earthtones. The yarn is an old standard, a worsted-weight wool, a practical, versatile yarn that takes dye beautifully.

For a pattern, I wanted something to reflect the curving and heavily textured nature of my vision. So, I researched old Aran Lace patterns again and came up with this one. I was unable to find a name for it, so I am just calling it Aran Lace. It uses extensive textural and stitch contrast, and I have combined it with a simple cable, but it is of only entry-level difficulty to knit, and it is still lace.

DESIGNING THE POTLUCK EARTHTONES COLORWAY

BY CHERYL POTTER

The Earthtones dye used here was one of the batches I tried and discarded when developing my African Gray colorway. The yarn I used is a standard worsted-weight, 100% wool called Potluck Worsted. It is both practical and inexpensive, a versatile and easy-to-handle fiber that also takes dye readily. This smooth, four-ply yarn is most often used for sweaters, hats, scarves, socks, mittens, or any garment designed for wear and tear. It is not a lace yarn, but like any yarn, can be used for lace. The yarn is packaged in what I call "six-packs." Each six-pack contains six 4-ounce hanks of yarn at 280 yards each, so there is enough yardage to produce a highly textured, generously sized piece that knits quickly on large needles.

Learning through Swatching

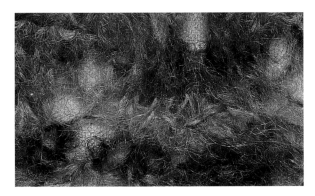

Brushed Mohair in Potluck Earthtones Colorway

This swatch is knit in Brushed Mohair in a similar Potluck Earthtones color. Although this yarn is considered worsted weight like the project yarn, the fact that it is brushed and therefore has a high nap dictates that it be knit on much larger needles. As seen here, even a size 10 needle does not help define the Aran Lace motif. The swatch knit on such a large needle shows neither pattern nor yarn to its best advantage. Because the mohair is so fuzzy, the pattern stitch is lost and the earthtone highlights of the Potluck color become obscured in the yarn. The result is a heather fabric with little detail. Although this is a typical scale with which to knit mohair, this combination is not suitable for this pattern because it renders it thin and uninteresting.

Learning Curve

Working with Potluck-colored yarn is the ultimate experience in lace knitting, no matter what the fiber, weight, or needle size. Because Potluck color can run rampant, it provides the perfect yarn to interpret a design idea on an individual level. Look at the myriad colors created on one hank or in a six-pack as a unique puzzle with many possible outcomes in a discrete space. Unlock the door to one color combination, and you find another possibility growing from the stitch pattern and the way the colors cross on the next row. This surprise becomes an exciting design element when creating lace and encourages a strong reaction in the interpretation of color and pattern. There is no wrong answer with Potluck yarn, only personal choice.

Technical Tips

This worsted-weight yarn is easy to work with as long as you maintain medium tension throughout the piece. Wool is a very forgiving fiber, but even so, keep in mind that the pattern is highly textured, which may vary in the tension from stitch to stitch. Try to keep an even hand.

The best and simplest technical advice for this project is to pay attention to what you are knitting. Use a counter to count rows and stitches and keep track of where you are in the pattern when you put the knitting aside.

Neither of us advocates mixing rows of various skeins of hand-painted yarn as most "experts" do, because we do not try to achieve an allover spread of color. Lace knitting tends to spread color in an organic way that does not require manipulating several balls at once. We also seek to glorify the uniqueness of each hank of yarn by creating a garment that looks different in various sections, like sun on leaves or sun among shadows.

Beginner's Edge

This design does not require fine technical skill, but it does require your undivided attention and careful counting. I hope the ebb and flow of this sinuous pattern will become automatic for new lace knitters. Try to get the hang of working the cable crosses by sight instead of following the chart line by line. The other pattern motif (chart A) is much harder to memorize completely, but you will find that you fall into a working rhythm as you knit.

I designed this stole so that it could double as a large head-and-neck wrap. You can customize it for your personal needs by knitting fewer repeats both horizontally and vertically. It makes a wonderfully warm, cuddly scarf with a look of complexity that belies its simple construction.

Finished Measurements

Approx 18" wide by 100" long after blocking

Materials

1 Cherry Tree Hill Inc. Potluck Worsted Wool Six-Pack (100% wool; 24 oz, 1680 yds per six-pack) in colorway Earthtones

Size US 7 (4.5 mm) needles or size to obtain gauge

Stitch markers

Medium-size cable needle

Gauge

Approx 4 sts and 4½ rows = 1" after blocking

Directions

Sl the first st of every row on the chart purlwise.

⁘ CO 80 sts and work 6 rows of garter st.

⁘ Beg horizontal patt layout on next RS row as follows: Work 4 sts of garter, PM, work 15 sts of chart A, PM, work 4 sts of chart B, PM, work 15 sts of chart A, PM, work 4 sts of chart B, PM, work 15 sts of chart A, PM, work 4 sts of chart B, PM, work 15 sts of chart A, PM, end with 4 sts of garter. Beg chart A on row 1 and work through row 8 while working cable patt at same time.

Note: The first eight rows of the Aran Lace pattern are the foundation for chart A and are not repeated after using them at the beginning. Chart A repeats from row 9 onward, so rows 9–22 are worked for the repeat. On chart B, after the first five rows, the cable crosses every four rows on the right side. It is important to note that you have a different repeat on each of the two motifs. When I knitted it, I kept track with a row counter for chart A and eyeballed chart B. If you find this too difficult, you can make a chart corresponding to the rows in the two patterns and then check off or cross through each combination as you finish that series of rows.

✤ Work until desired length, ending on row 14 of chart A. Work 6 rows of garter st. BO loosely.

Blocking

Soak stole overnight in cold water without soap. Place in spin cycle of washer to remove excess moisture. Lay on flat surface and pull into desired dimensions while wet. Pins are not necessary. When dry, weave in ends.

Chart A: Aran Lace Pattern
15-st horizontal pattern
14-row vertical rep; 7 rows to start
Note: Not all rows have the same number of sts.

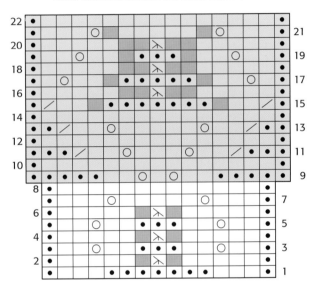

Work rows 1–8 once, then rep rows 9–22 for patt. End last rep with completed row 14.

Chart B: Cable Pattern
4-st horizontal pattern
4-row vertical rep

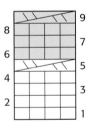

Make first cross on row 5, and then make cross on every 4th row.

☐	K on RS, P on WS
•	P on RS, K on WS
○	YO
╱	P2tog
⋏	Sl 1 pw, P2tog, psso
▨	No stitch
⬚	Sl 2 sts to cn, hold at back, K2, K2 from cn.

Rainstorm and Desert Dusk

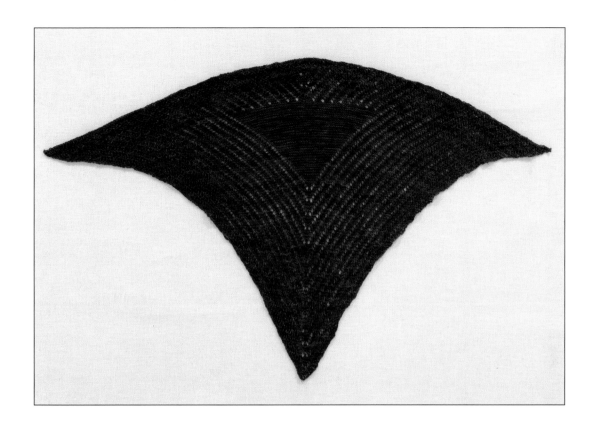

Designing the Project

BY CAROL RASMUSSEN NOBLE

THIS DESIGN BEGAN with a sunset colorway in which the rich hues run toward the fuchsia of sunset and back again toward the darkening greens and blues of dusk. It reminded me of the sky at sunset near my Nevada desert home after an intense rainstorm—dark but vivid colors lit by low light at the horizon. In the desert, the sky never appears stormy all over because the vista is so wide. Instead, thunderheads and rain are visible in their entirety, occupying part of a vast sky off in the distance. Colors in the air look saturated because of the clarity of light, present nowhere else but in the desert Southwest.

I approached the design of this shawl from a different perspective than I have used in previous projects. I decided on three predetermined elements and challenged myself to make a multi-faceted pattern for them that would grow into different shapes as the shawl moved upward. The first given was the color: a colorway called Dusk, noted for saturated hues of deep sapphire, emerald, purple, and fuchsia. The second given was the fiber: Supersock Merino, a fingering-weight two-ply Superwash sock yarn with a tight, glossy twist that is both durable and elastic. This machine-washable yarn is ideal to experiment with in patterning, because it knits up cleanly and shows a textured pattern well. I chose size 4 (3.5 mm) needles and found the yarn forgiving. Pattern stitches are easy to see, and the fabric is easy to rip out if need be.

57

Rain Line and Reverse Rain Line are simple
motifs, which form the building blocks
of this allover patterned shawl.

Garter areas form the third motif, Clouds,
from which the Rain Lines originate.

The last given was the shape: a triangle. Working within its outlines, I wanted to suggest the illusion of massive storm clouds sending down driving rain. The pattern I created has no particular provenance and is married from disparate elements. It originates from a simple four-stitch repeat—K2, K2tog, YO—which when knit forms a slanting vertical line that I named a Rain Line for purposes of this design. When alternated with plain garter reverse-side rows, Rain Line motifs move in a diagonal line to the right of the center-back pattern column. To the left of the center back, they slant in the opposite direction, upward toward the left, and are reversed into YO, SSK, K2. For the purposes of this pattern, I call this left-slanting-line motif a Reverse Rain Line. The effect is that the motifs look as if they grow from a center-back column that is patterned in its own right. The pattern of the center back is a column of boxy shapes formed by areas of garter stitch from which the Rain Line motifs grow. Each mirrored set of slanting lines has a boxy area of garter stitch connecting its base up to the base of the next set of mirrored slanting lines. I call these boxy garter-stitch areas Clouds for the purposes of this pattern.

As the design progresses, 14 sets of mirrored Rain Lines form at the top of this column of 14 Clouds, the patterning stops, and the center back blooms into a large triangle with diagonal-line motifs at the edges. I see this triangle as a huge storm cloud.

Close-Up of Center Triangle in Shawl

Unlike any lacework I have done thus far, these three basic motifs morph in and out of each other to build the overall pattern. At the same time, yarn overs are worked at the beginning and end of every right-side row to give additional fullness in shaping the triangle. When the interior center triangle becomes large enough to accommodate an even repeat of Rain Lines and Clouds along the top, the pattern reverts to that of the area below the large triangle and is worked in the same manner. Lines branch from a center-back area to the right and left with their bases in the large triangle. In other words, one set of Rain Lines grows from the center and then in each direction along the top edge. The curve of the shawl's lacy edge is created from a difference in tension between the solid garter triangle and the Rain Line motifs to either side and is an attractive addition. I would like to acknowledge the help of my lace mentor, Margaret Peterson, of Unst, Shetland, with this design.

DESIGNING THE DUSK COLORWAY

BY CHERYL POTTER

From time to time, I hold colorway contests to discover what the knitting public craves in terms of dye combinations. Anyone can send in an idea in any medium: I have received Crayola drawings, colored Easter Eggs, ranges of hand-made chocolates and palettes of shaded embroidery thread, to name a few! From the hundreds of entries a few years back, I was most intrigued by a colorway labeled Dusk. Unlike the darkening shades it suggests, this sequence was arranged in saturated hues that ran toward a central color, and then away. I came to call this a sunset colorway. I love the idea of colors growing deep and overtaking the horizon in a splashy show just before being lost to twilight. The shading of greens to brilliant blue, amethyst, and burgundy captured that for me here.

Learning through Swatching

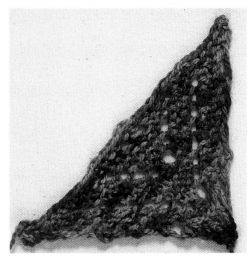

8-ply New Zealand Wool in Dusk Colorway

This swatch is knit with an eight-ply (DK) New Zealand 100% wool yarn, also shown in the colorway Dusk. It is DK weight, which is heavier than Supersock Merino. Although it must be knit on larger needles and is not washable, it does provide an alternative for knitters who desire a quick-knit shawl, albeit thicker, stiffer, and with less drape. Like the Supersock, the New Zealand Wool takes the color brilliantly and shows the pattern motif clearly.

Learning Curve

Lace does not need to consist of several singular and discrete motifs used separately, but can actually grow—one pattern directly from another—to suggest a multifaceted design idea. Even simple patterns, as in this project, can progress to create elegant and effective lace garments. Rather than detracting, the hand-painted colorway only enhances the appeal. This is a prime opportunity for novice chart users to sharpen their chart-reading skills. Although the three design motifs introduced in this project combine to form a complex image, they use entry-level knitting skills in this yarn and scale. The combination represents my vision of a stormy sky with rain pelting from deep clouds. Although it looks complicated, the design is not fussy or overwrought like many of the currently available shawl patterns featuring multiple motifs. Another difference is that here, the three motif areas are related, forming a cohesive design than cannot be broken into parts without destroying the whole. The patterns unite into an integrated whole instead of existing as separate, competing elements.

Technical Tips

Work with medium to light tension, as tightness will cause unevenness over the surface of the shawl because of the difference in stitch types. Also, the yarn has a high twist and should not be stretched as it is knit, or it will tend to resist flatness in the finished fabric.

Slip the first stitch purlwise at the beginning of each row—even though it is followed by a yarn over—to preserve the hint of laciness built into the edges of the shawl. To achieve the proper twist on the Rain Line motif and to maintain an even surface on the Cloud pattern, it is important to use a small needle size, even if it appears as though the knitting would progress more easily on a larger needle. Make sure that all areas of the shawl have even, balanced stitches. It is harder than you might think to knit an even garter stitch, but practice makes perfect.

Beginner's Edge

Side edges will have a tendency to pull in and the top edges to curve, but this tendency is a part of the finished look of the shawl and should not be vigorously blocked out. This garment was designed as a head or shoulder scarf. To make it larger, work more repeats before starting the center triangle in chart D, and make the center triangle larger in proportion.

Remember that the Rain Lines are only a four-stitch repeat radiating symmetrically out from the center, as shown on charts A through C. Do not feel overwhelmed at the outset by seemingly difficult directions. Once you generate the first cloud, what follows will become apparent visually and rhythmically. This is the perfect project for learning how to read simple charts that both reverse at the centerline and morph into each other.

Finished Measurements

(after blocking)

Center back: 29"
Width at top edge: 53"

Materials

2 hanks of Cherry Tree Hill Inc. Supersock Merino (100% merino; 4 oz, 370 yds per hank) in colorway Dusk

Size US 4 (3.5 mm) needles or size to obtain gauge

Stitch markers

Blocking T pins

Gauge

Approx 4 sts and 6 rows = 1" in pattern after blocking

Directions

Sl the first of every row purlwise.

Note: The pattern is shown from the point up in progressive charts for various sections. New chart readers need to take note that only the repeat of each chart is indicated. For example, the entire repeat of the Rain Lines is not shown because it would be redundant. It merely continues across, as shown in the chart, as K2, K2tog, YO on the right of the centerline, and YO, SSK, K2 on the left of the centerline. Make sure the centerline is clearly marked with stitch markers. Note that patterning occurs only on right-side rows. All wrong-side rows are knit.

❖ CO 3 sts, and beg chart A, working rows 1–10. Work charts B and C, which are actually identical at the center. Cont in patt until there are 13 completed reps of the small Cloud motif at the center back. Beg chart D, filling in the center with solid stitches, and cont the Rain Lines up the edges of the shawl. As you discontinue new Rain Lines, you will see a solid triangle of knitting growing at the center of the garment. Knit in patt until there are 65 sts along top edge of solid triangle, ending with completed WS row.

✣ On next RS row, knit in established patt to first st of large triangle. Then work Rain Line motif (K2, K2tog, YO) 7 times. At center back, K3, YO, K1, YO, K3, then work Reverse Rain Line motif (YO, SSK, K2) 7 times, cont across top in established patt.

✣ Work 4½ reps of chart C, with center back in center of patt as shown below triangle. BO very loosely.

Blocking

Soak shawl overnight in cold water without soap. Then run through the spin cycle of washer to remove excess moisture. Lay out on flat surface and pin edges with moderate tension. This project has a lot of stretch, so you can block to taste. I recommend a medium block to allow ease for drape when the shawl is worn.

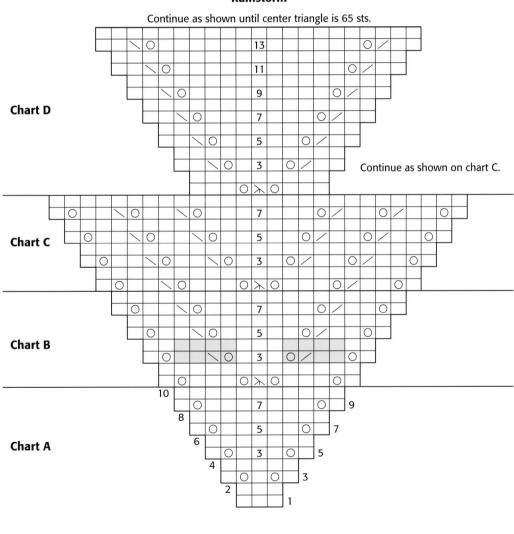

Rainstorm

Continue as shown until center triangle is 65 sts.

Chart D

Continue as shown on chart C.

Chart C

Chart B

Chart A

	K on both sides		/	K2tog
O	YO		\	SSK
⋌	Sl 1, K2tog, psso		3	Numbers indicate sts between YO

Patt rep for left rain line

Patt rep for right rain line

A Season of Mists and Mellow Fruitfulness

Designing the Project

BY CAROL RASMUSSEN NOBLE

KEATS'S POEM "TO AUTUMN" is one of my favorites for the sheer perfection of his vision. In my mind, it is synonymous with the colorway Indian Summer and was the first thing I thought of when I saw the blend of harvest shades Cheryl designed.

I looked for a pattern or patterns that would in some way reflect Indian summer as the colorway did. I decided on Shetland Small Trees and Shetland Diamonds, two distinct patterns combined to form one. With the tree motif and the diamonds as fallen leaves on cut fields, I found expression for my idea. This is another way to morph designs, but unlike the pattern in the last chapter, the patterns here do not grow and change out of one another; they simply lock together like a jigsaw puzzle to form a larger picture. The yarn I chose was the first true lace yarn in this book—Suri Lace. Although Suri Lace was previously sampled for swatching, this is the first time I have selected it for a finished project.

Although this fragile two-ply yarn does not have a high nap, it lofts when knit and becomes fuzzy, not unlike kid mohair. This featherweight yarn is very warm when knit and provides a luxurious and exotic fabric.

DESIGNING THE INDIAN SUMMER COLORWAY

BY CHERYL POTTER

Unlike other combinations of autumn colorways such as Fall Foliage, Indian Summer is a mellower sequence for me. Rather than symbolizing the sugar maples and crisp mornings with sharp colors like bright amethyst and deep orange, I saw instead a cornucopia of root vegetables. In my mind's eye, turnip and parsnip and butternut squash and pumpkin still on the vine lay gathered before a stand of sunbleached corn and patches of Indian paintbrush and black-eyed Susans.

Learning through Swatching

Swatch 1: Kid Mohair Lace in
Indian Summer Colorway

I chose to swatch the Shetland Small Trees and Shetland Diamond patterns in the same color-way—Indian Summer—but with a slightly different yarn, Kid Mohair Lace. The difference between the Suri Lace and the Kid Mohair is the animal. While Suri Lace originates from alpaca, Kid Mohair originates from baby angora goat. Kid Mohair is softer and less hairy than its better-known, worsted-weight brushed mohair counterpart, and it tends to fuzz more. Lace-weight Kid Mohair is a viable alternative for those who do not wish to tackle a more exotic and delicate yarn like Suri Lace, but the trade-off is that the Kid Mohair lacks the hand and the superlight airiness of the alpaca. Another drawback is that the fuzziness of the mohair obscures the pattern motifs, which are not simple enough to be defined by brushed mohair. Nevertheless, the Kid Mohair would provide a lovely, inexpensive medium-weight shawl, although somewhat coarser.

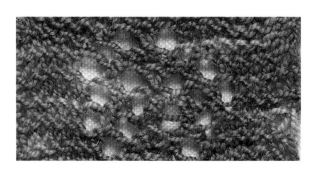

Swatch 2: Supersock Merino in
Indian Summer Colorway

This swatch is shown in a thicker fingering-weight yarn, Supersock Merino, also in the same colorway, Indian Summer. Although this is also a two-ply yarn, it has a much tighter twist, and because it is Superwash, it takes the color much more brightly than a hand-wash yarn like alpaca. Overall, the merino proved too bulky for the effect I wished to achieve in this shawl. Compared to the other two yarns sampled, Supersock Merino lacks the airiness of the Suri Lace and the luxury feel of the Kid Mohair. The two Shetland motifs I have chosen are too fine for this yarn, although the high twist ensures it would define them nicely. As seen in the previous project, Supersock Merino works well in shawls, but makes a bolder statement on a larger scale than I wish to make in this garment.

Learning Curve

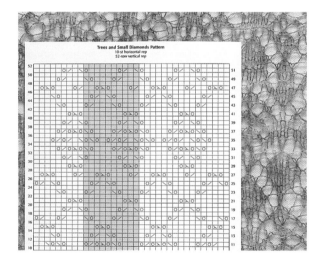

Like a jigsaw puzzle, the chart shows how the
two motifs fit together, but once knit up in a stole,
all you see is a design that is an organic whole.

I hope lace knitters come away from this project with a new approach to patterning. As a lesson in overall graphing, the most obvious new technique learned in this project is how to knit single patterns in combination with each other in an interlocked way. A study of the charts reveals that one motif fits into the other like a puzzle piece, resulting in an overall design that resembles a broad pattern stripe.

To approach this type of designing as an exercise, take an allover grid in bands of one to three repeats and begin filling in a secondary pattern, which should be a simple individual motif, in the blank spaces between the repeats of the primary motifs. The simplest way to graph new combinations is by filling in pattern stripes; another easy way is to draw filler patterns in the centers of the diamond grids. I chose a simple pattern stripe against a diamond grid, as seen in the chart, offset by the second pattern stripe so that the motifs do not appear to line up in columns. Graphing sounds much harder than it is. I hope this will provide the visual clarity you require to begin creating your own patterns by combining simple motifs as I did in this project.

Technical Tips

Another skill learned in this project is how to handle a finicky lace yarn. Although Suri Lace is two-ply yarn, the plies are slightly fuzzy and not tightly twisted, making it a delicate yarn to knit. Try a sample swatch first to get the feel of it— Suri Lace is stretchy, splits and rubs away easily, and takes tension unevenly if you are not careful. The good news is that irregularities are easily blocked out. Knit Suri Lace with a careful hand and a moderately light tension. Refrain from pulling on it in the knitting stage; leave that for the blocking stage where it will be needed.

Please note that the stitches and especially the yarn overs like to escape the needles; if they do, you will have a terrible mess. Keep track of stitches and do any repairs immediately. The yarn is ruined by ripping out and cannot be reknit. Do not despair! By now, you are a seasoned lace knitter who possesses the skills this project requires. The shawl may not knit up quickly, but in the end, you will own a gorgeous piece of hand-knit lace that is lighter than air. The pattern is not difficult and the yarn is manageable if worked with care. Learning how to handle this yarn correctly requires knitting it. The resultant shawl is akin to wearing a cloud of pale harvest mist.

Beginner's Edge

Traditional lace requires more intermediate skill, yet I feel that the skills learned in the first 10 projects will serve you well here. Follow your instincts, treat the yarn delicately, and remember that the motifs themselves are relatively simple. There is a lot of stretch in this yarn, so after blocking, the pattern will be much clearer as well as very light and airy. Trust yourself and experiment.

Finished Measurements

Approx 26" by 80" after blocking

Materials

2 hanks of Cherry Tree Hill Inc. Suri Lace (100% Suri alpaca; 50 g, 437 yds per hank) in colorway Indian Summer

Size US 2 (2.75 mm) needles or size to obtain gauge

Stitch markers

Blocking T pins

Gauge

Approx 4 sts and 5¼ rows = 1" in pattern after blocking

Directions

Sl the first st of every row purlwise; count this st as one of the garter edge sts.

❖ CO 103 sts and work 6 rows of garter st.

❖ Beg horizontal patt layout on next RS row as follows: Work 4 sts in garter, PM, referring to chart, work 16 beg sts, PM, work 10-st patt rep 7 times (PM between each patt rep), PM, work 9 end sts, PM, end with 4 sts in garter.

❖ Work 52-row vertical rep a total of 8 times, followed by rows 1–16 to balance the patt at the ends of the stole so they end in the same pattern stripe. Work 6 rows of garter st. BO very loosely.

Blocking

Soak shawl overnight in cold water without soap. Roll into a towel to gently squeeze out moisture. Block tautly and scallop the edges with pins.

Do not be afraid to pull hard; the alpaca will not tear. Leave blocked on a flat surface out of the sun until thoroughly dry, plus one day to set after drying. Unpin and enjoy.

Trees and Small Diamonds Pattern
10-st horizontal rep
52-row vertical rep

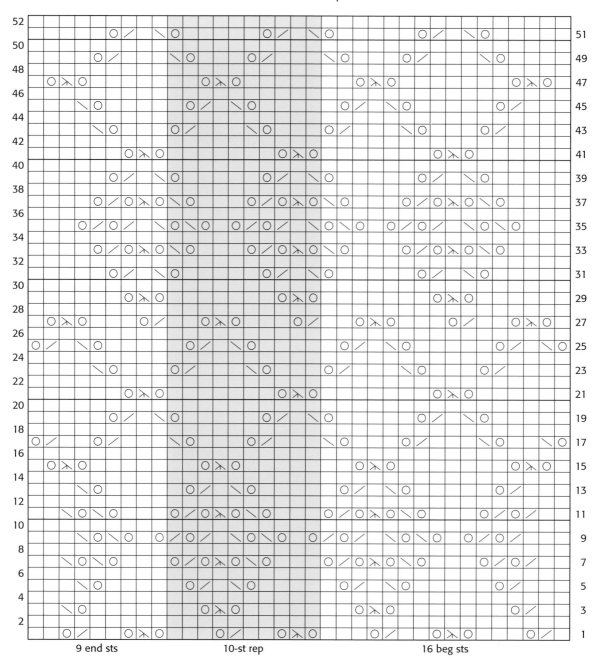

9 end sts   10-st rep   16 beg sts

	K on both sides		K2tog
	YO		SSK
	Sl 1 kw, K2tog, psso		

Rosebuds and Climbing Roses

Designing the Project

BY CAROL RASMUSSEN NOBLE

WHEN I WAS A VERY SMALL CHILD, my grandfather grew roses. He has been gone a long time now, but I can still remember his garden in my child's eye: a profusion of blooms on bushes and trellises, shades of pink and reds, all with a well-cultivated wildness.

To reproduce the vision of my grandfather's garden, I chose Merino Lace, a lovely lace-weight wool that knits up to medium thickness in lace terms and softens and glows after dyeing and blocking. The colorway I chose is Cheryl's Wild Cherry, an exuberant blend of the colors in my memory.

Keeping with the main idea, I wanted to make a traditional Shetland stole using two patterns, so I chose in a very pictorial way the Rosebud for the center section and Trellis Diamond for the ends. The traditional Shetland stole has one pattern that is used at each end of the rectangle. The center section, which is twice as long as one of the end sections, uses a different pattern. Lace holes are often used at the pattern changes as I have done here. The only traditional element lacking in this somewhat scaled-down design is a knitted-on scalloped border.

DESIGNING THE WILD CHERRY COLORWAY

BY CHERYL POTTER

I have similar memories of a garden, only it was my grandmother's flower garden bordering the side of an old white farmhouse. I recall racing with abandon through the rows of pink lady slipper and lilac, lush under a sunny turquoise sky in early summer. My grandmother would be at the side door calling me for lunch and I would crouch in the daffodils, pretend not to hear, all the while giggling in the greenery. This image later became the inspiration for another of my colorways: Country Garden.

While a perfectly usable colorway, Country Garden did not speak of roses or the sense of cultivated wildness that Carol wished to portray. Designer and dyer settled on a subtler colorway with a hint of natural abandon, Wild Cherry, which is dyed in multicolored reds, pink, and hints of mulberry and burgundy. This colorway came to me unexpectedly, as I happened across a forgotten orchard while hiking an old logging trail through the woods of Vermont. The trees, though long gone wild, stood in a semblance of rows and still bore fruit. There was a sense of old order and the simple pleasures of days gone by that remained with me long after I left the magical orchard. It was this sense of nostalgia that I wanted to bring to Carol's design.

Learning through Swatching

Suri Lace in Wild Cherry Colorway

This swatch is shown in an alpaca, lace-weight yarn knitters have had many opportunities to familiarize themselves with thus far: Suri Lace. Although it is shown in the same colorway as the project yarn, the alpaca takes the Wild Cherry dyes in a subtler way. The swatch is knit in the same pattern motif with the same needle size as the project yarn, and the result is a wonderful alternative for more confident lace knitters. The Suri Lace knits into an airy and delicate lace stole, while the Merino Lace is easier to knit, more substantial, and a less expensive luxury yarn.

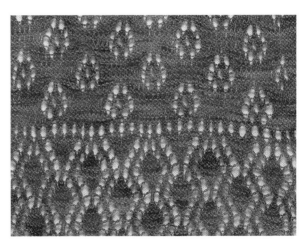

A row of lace holes separates the
Trellis Diamond and Rosebud patterns.

Learning Curve

This project introduces designing and knitting a traditional garment from the Shetland Islands using lace-weight yarn. Like the previous shawl, two or more patterns are knit into sections of lace. The key is balance. Shetlanders teach that the center of the stole, which will be the portion laid across the back, should portray a simpler and denser design than the pattern on the ends, which are visible on the chest. Ends are reserved for exhibiting more complicated or openwork motifs. In this project, the simpler Rosebud pattern is worked in the middle, balanced by the vertically oriented and more open pattern of Trellis Diamonds on the ends. The key to this project is the concept of balancing open and closed spaces in a series of panels, using different motifs within the same garment.

Technical Tips

Merino Lace does not exhibit as much stretch as many lace-weight yarns. It knits up tightly, so use relaxed tension, especially when patterning. Make certain to maintain shape and size between pattern areas.

Beginner's Edge

Balancing open and closed spaces helps to coordinate patterns so that they feel right together. Watch your tension closely and be prepared to modify as you move from one pattern area to the next. Maintaining width evenly in different sections of pattern motif is essential, as this yarn has little elasticity and will not allow you to block out a large difference in width between sections.

Finished Measurements

Approx 13" wide by 56" long after blocking

Materials

1 hank Cherry Tree Hill Inc. Merino Lace (100% merino wool; 8 oz, 2400 yds per hank) in colorway Wild Cherry

Size US 2 (2.75 mm) needles or size to obtain gauge

Stitch markers

Blocking T pins

Gauge

7½ sts and 7 rows =1" in pattern after blocking

Directions

Sl the first st of every row purlwise; count this st as one of the seed edge sts.

Seed Stitch
Row 1 (RS): K1, P1 across.
Row 2 (WS): P1, K1 across.

❖ CO 99 stitches and work 8 rows of seed st, followed by 2 rows of garter st.

❖ Beg horizontal patt layout on next RS row for chart A is as follows: Work 8 seed sts, PM, work 5 garter sts, PM, referring to chart, work 12 beg sts, PM, work 12-st patt rep 4 times (PM between each patt rep), PM, work 13 end sts, PM, work 5 garter sts and PM, end with 8 seed sts. Knit all WS rows except for seed-st sections.

❖ Work 12-row vertical rep from chart A total of 8 times.

❖ While maintaining the 8-st seed-st border as established, work 2 rows of garter st, 2 rows of chart B, followed by 2 rows of garter st, dec 2 sts on last row—97 sts. You are now ready for chart C.

❖ Beg horizontal patt layout on next RS row for chart B as follows: Work 6 seed sts, PM, work 7 beg sts, 16-st patt rep 4 times (PM between each patt rep), PM, work 14 end sts, PM, work 6 seed sts.

❖ Work 16-row vertical rep from chart C a total of 11 times, then work rows 1–10, increasing 2 sts on row 10—99 sts.

❖ Work 2 rows of garter st, 2 rows of chart B, and 2 rows of garter st. You are now prepared for chart A again.

❖ Work chart A as previously directed, working 12-row vertical rep a total of 8 times.

❖ Work 2 rows of garter st, followed by 8 rows of seed st. BO very loosely.

Blocking

Soak stole overnight in cold water without soap. Roll in a towel to press out excess moisture and block with medium tension using pins. Allow to remain blocked one day after dry to set pattern.

Chart A: Trellis Diamond Pattern
12-st horizontal rep
12-row vertical rep

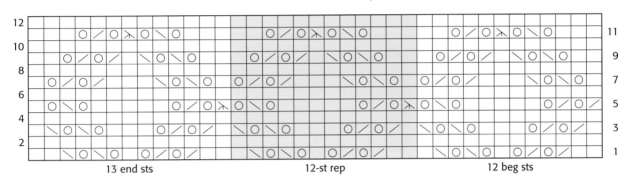

13 end sts   12-st rep   12 beg sts

Chart B: Lace Holes
2-st horizontal rep
2-row vertical rep

2-st rep
1 edge st

Chart C: Rosebud Pattern
16-st horizontal rep
16-row vertical rep

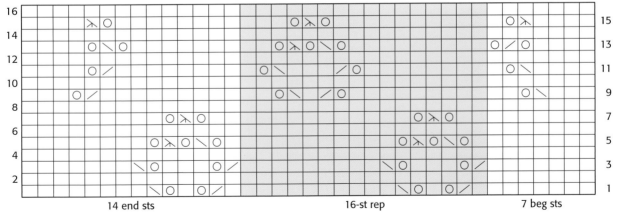

14 end sts   16-st rep   7 beg sts

Note: There is a delayed decrease on row 15 in the end motifs. Rows 13 and 14 will have 8 sts in the beg sts and 15 sts in the end sts. Sts will revert back to normal on row 15.

	K on both sides		K2tog
	YO		SSK
	Sl 1 kw, K2tog, psso		

Frost Flowers

Designing the Project

BY CAROL RASMUSSEN NOBLE

THE SCENE IS deep winter on the shores of Lake Superior: pale, northern winter light glitters through the frost flowers growing on my window, creating shimmering pastels of ice—color that is more light than color. This picture is what I saw when I looked at a skein of Cascade fingering-weight silk in Cheryl's colorway Spring Frost.

It was such a strong visual impression that I cannot say anything more about it as far as process goes. It was as if the yarn were calling to me, telling me what it wanted to be.

Almost a noncolor, this colorway in silk requires a more solid fabric with fewer holes to shine to advantage. For this reason, I chose the Shetland Fern Lace stitch with its meandering vines and leaves, separated by lace-hole diamonds for the center. To me these patterns represented the winding frost flowers I saw on my window.

DESIGNING THE SPRING FROST COLORWAY
BY CHERYL POTTER

The colors conjure an image of an early childhood morning in Maine. I recall feeling the absolute cold of the frozen house, breathing on the window glass of a front door frosted over with white, and seeing the thin rays of sun trying to penetrate. As my breath melted the frost, the sun glittered through and I saw a winter rainbow of peach and lavender and silver as the sun touched the snow.

When this image was translated into fiber, it became clear that the alpaca previously used would not capture the image of sun burning through frost, as there was no shine. To exploit the colors of Spring Frost and enhance our twin images of a wintry morning, I chose for Carol a two-ply silk called Cascade Fingering.

Learning through Swatching

Suri Lace and Superwash Worsted Yarn Samples

The headline for this section could easily be "No Swatch Needed." Both sample yarns are shown in the project colorway, Spring Frost, but tend to distort the colorway in different ways. The first yarn sample is Suri Lace, which I have used successfully several times. This is a very fine yarn unsuited for large, close areas. Like the project yarn, it is muted and has some depth, but the fuzziness distorts color separation in this delicate colorway, making it seem more water colored than it is and less interesting. The other sample is Superwash Worsted, a four-ply 100% merino yarn. It pulls and separates the colors of Spring Frost, lending it toneless colors with high contrast more suitable for a baby blanket in some other lace stitch with more holes to separate the color.

Time and time again, we encourage beginning lace knitters to swatch, swatch, swatch. Throughout this book, we both have enjoyed breaking "rules" of lace knitting and you may wonder: Are we at last breaking even our own rules? As rules are made to be broken, the answer here is a qualified "yes." We both feel that it would be futile to show examples of other yarns knit in the Frost Flower pattern, because this scarf is an example of a design in which the yarn is married to the pattern. This is not uncommon in the design world. For example, recall that for many sock patterns, only fingering-weight sock yarn is recommended, and think of all the Fair Isle sweater designs that call for Shetland wool only.

In this silk scarf, the colorway as seen on this one yarn is an element integral to the piece. Please recall that the yarn has much to say about how the colorway presents itself. As seen here, other yarns take this delicate colorway in very different ways. We both feel that no other combination of stitch pattern, fiber, and colorway could come near to duplicating the beauty of this piece. As an integral whole, it is the culmination of all we have revealed and the ultimate exercise of our book.

Learning Curve

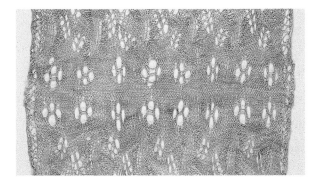

A row of lace holes is worked from a provisional cast on before the Fern Lace pattern is started.

This project introduces a new technique called the provisional center cast on. To begin, cast on stitches in waste yarn and work two rows of garter stitch. Then break the waste yarn and join the project yarn without tying on and work four rows of garter. This is the center of the scarf—the pattern is knit from center to end on both sides and then bound off. After binding off the first side, turn the work so that the cast-on edge is at the top. Snip and discard the waste, then slip the lace yarn stitches onto a needle, with the point facing the tail of the yarn. Now the scarf is ready to complete by knitting the other end of the piece out from the center.

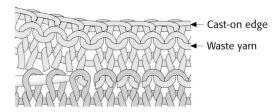

◄ Cast-on edge
◄ Waste yarn

Technical Tips

This scarf has a herringbone edge that is knit differently on the right and wrong sides, so follow chart B carefully. This lace edge continues for the entire length of the piece, so it must be started at each edge right after the provisional cast on.

Be careful to cross yarn overs properly in the herringbone motif, as it is easy to confuse them. All four edges will be knit from center to end.

Tension is no problem here as silk is easy to knit and has little stretch. Try to choose a waste yarn no thicker than the project yarn so that the edge does not stretch out in the center. I used a Shetland two-ply yarn for the cast on in this piece. Also, make certain you knit the two ends with both right sides facing up and both wrong sides facing down. If you make a mistake, it is possible to knit an extra row of garter before beginning the pattern. The center provisional cast on is meant to give a smooth, joinless fabric.

Beginner's Edge

We have taken you on a previously uncharted journey through the world of lace knitting and hope you are the more adventuresome knitter for it. We began with Ocean Moods, which introduced you to a typical vision of traditional lace, and then began breaking all the rules. We knit lace with yarns, fibers, and colors no one has tried before. We knit lace with unheard-of needle sizes and unique techniques and revealed little-known tricks of the trade to feed your comfort level. We led you through the pitfalls, encouraged you to make your own way, and now we have come full circle in this last project to a more complex lace design that is both traditional and yet startlingly novel in color.

This project carries with it the whole wealth of what has come before and returns you to the beginning point of exquisite lace, but without the stereotypes. Remember that lace is not just your grandmother's tablecloth. Rather than daunting or tedious, lace—especially hand-painted lace—is an experience of discovery in which the colors combine and recombine, row by row. Lace holes spread the color. Garter ground concentrates it. Lace can be a practical shawl or a wearable scarf. As the purest form of knitting and design, lace can be whatever you want it to be.

Finished Measurements

Approx 15" wide by 48" long after blocking

Materials

1 hank of Cherry Tree Hill Inc. Cascade Fingering
Silk (100% silk; 150 g, 666 yds per hank) in
colorway Spring Frost

Size US 2 (2.75 mm) needles or size to obtain
gauge

Stitch markers

Blocking T pins

Gauge

Approx 7 sts and 5¼ rows = 1" after blocking

Directions

Sl the first st of every row purlwise.

❖ CO 104 sts with waste yarn and work 2 rows
of garter st. Join lace yarn without tying on
and work 4 rows of garter st.

❖ *Beg horizontal layout on next RS row as follows: Work 6 right-edge sts of chart B, PM,
from chart C work 10 beg sts, PM, work 12-st
patt rep 6 times (PM between each patt rep),
PM, work 10 end sts, PM, work 6 left-edge sts
of chart B. Work 6-row vertical patt rep from
chart C once while at same time working left

and right patts of chart B. After working lace-
hole diamonds on chart C, cont with both
edges for chart B and work 4 more rows of
garter st, ending with completed WS row.

❖ On next RS row, beg horizontal patt rep for
chart A as follows: Work 6 right-edge sts of
chart B, PM, work 11 beg sts from chart A,
PM, work 18-st patt rep 4 times (PM between
each patt rep), PM, work 9 end sts, PM, end
with 6 left-edge sts from chart B.

❖ Work 12-row vertical rep from chart A total
of 10 times, ending with completed WS row.
While maintaining herringbone edge patts,
work 4 rows of garter st. BO loosely.

❖ Turn piece so that waste CO is at top, pre-
sented for knitting. Carefully snip away and
discard waste yarn and slip live stitches to a
needle with point facing yarn tails. Work 3
rows of garter st. Work from * at beg of patt,
following directions as for first half of scarf.

Blocking

Soak scarf overnight in cold water without soap.
Roll into a towel to press out excess moisture.
Block on a flat surface at light to moderate tension, with special attention to straight edges. You
may need to pull one part of the scarf more than
another to achieve this. Remember that blocking
restores shine in a piece that has been handled a
lot. When you unpin the scarf, knead it slightly to
rid it of the stiffness left by blocking.

Chart A: Fern Lace Pattern
18-st horizontal rep
12-row vertical rep

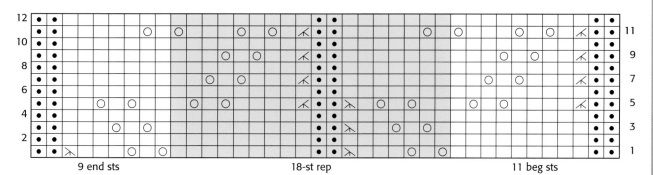

9 end sts   18-st rep   11 beg sts

Chart B: Herringbone Edges
6-st horizontal rep
2-row vertical rep

Right edge   Left edge

6-st rep   6-st rep

Chart C: Lace-Hole Diamonds
12-st horizontal rep
6-row vertical rep

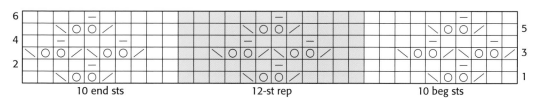

10 end sts   12-st rep   10 beg sts

☐	K on both sides
•	P on RS, K on WS
—	P on WS
O	YO
×	Sl 1 at beg of row, K at end of row
/	K2tog
\	SSK
⋌	Sl 1 kw, K2tog, psso
⋏	K3tog

Frost Flowers

The dye methods described below are given in order from the simplest to the most complex. All of these methods fall into the category of hand-painted yarn.

Immersion Dye

The immersion-dye technique is simple: just immerse an entire hank of yarn in dye solution. The term *immersion dye* is often mistakenly called *hand dye*, a misnomer, since *hand dye* can refer to a number of different dye methods. Both terms are often used to indicate monochromatic dyeing. This results in a semisolid color range that can be striking or barely discernible, depending upon the manipulation of the yarn in the dye bath. The advantage of knitting with this type of yarn is that you can knit it as you would a solid, and it is especially suited to detailed pattern stitches.

Dip Dye

The dip-dye method is slightly more involved than the immersion dye. Here, different sections of a dye skein are dipped in several different dye baths, either simultaneously or consecutively. Dip-dyed yarn features multicolored repeats in long color stretches in which colors merge with neighboring colors to create new ones along the same length of yarn. This yarn loves to be knit multidirectionally. It is especially effective with insertion-lace projects; diagonal knitting, such as triangular shawls; and side-to-side pieces.

Space Dye

The space-dye method is the most common technique and is commonly referred to as *hand paint*, another misnomer, since *hand paint* can mean any yarn painted by hand. *Space dye* means to dye a hank of yarn in a colorway, or certain sequence, which is repeatable from hank to hank. Usually several yarns are dyed together in a colorway, and these become a dye lot of that space-dyed combination. Space-dyed yarns are known for multicolored repeats of short color stretches in which colors merge with neighboring colors to produce new and interesting combinations. Spaced-dyed yarns are especially suited to lace knitting, which often uses garter stitch and small knit-purl combinations for dramatic effect. Lace holes highlight space-dyed yarns by spreading the many colors even farther, offering a mosaic look.

Hand Paint

This term literally means to paint fiber by hand, usually with brushes or squirt bottles. The multicolored dyes are applied randomly and there is no colorway or repeat. Be aware that, in recent times, *hand paint* has become an overused catch-all phrase meaning any kind of hand-processed fiber with a painted look. With hand paints, colors are applied randomly on a dye skein to merge with their neighbors at will, so that many secondary and tertiary colors are created. Hand-painted hanks need strong designs to exploit the rich spread of color, which make these yarns perfect for lace knitting. The lace holes and multidirectional designs, characteristic of lace, break up and recombine hand-painted yarns, providing lace fabric with a designer look.

Potluck

Potluck is a dye term I coined more than ten years ago and it means "luck of the dye pot." The idea came to me from fond memories of potluck suppers so popular when I was a child, when families would bring a covered dish to a church or picnic and you never knew what delicious combination would be hiding under the lid. Potluck yarn works the same way. Instead of sequencing a colorway in which the spread of dye is controlled, colors are applied liberally or not, once or many times, depending upon the look the dyer wants to achieve. Each Potluck batch is unique and impossible to replicate.

Here, the idea of hand painting is taken to a new level as yarns are painted, manipulated in a pot of hot water, and then left to cool overnight. As the temperature drops, the fiber absorbs the dyes at a slower rate. This creates one-of-a-kind multicolors that contrast by depth and shade. Many of the colors do not penetrate through the hank, adding to the random quality, and some colors become heathered or shaded as they combine during the cooling process. Potluck hanks are the most exciting yarns to work with while patterning lace. Simple lace motifs are highlighted by the striking color changes, and garments shimmer with the movement of color.

Abbreviations and Glossary

approx	approximately
beg	beginning
BO	bind off
CO	cast on
cont	continue
dec	decrease
g	grams
garter ground	knit every row
inc	increase
K	knit
K2tog	knit two stiches together
m	meter
M1	make one stitch
oz	ounces

P	purl
patt(s)	pattern(s)
PM	place marker
psso	pass slipped stitch(es) over
pw	purlwise
rep	repeat
RS	right side
sl st	slip stitch
SSK	slip two stitches separately as if to knit, insert the left needle into the front of the two stitches from left to right and knit the two stitches together.
st(s)	stitch(es)

St st	stockinette stitch
stockinette ground	knit on right side, purl on wrong side
WS	wrong side
yds	yards
YO	yarn over

Yarn Conversion Chart

yds x 0.9144 = m
m x 1.0936 = yds
g x 0.0352 = oz
oz x 28.35 = g

Resources

Cherry Tree Hill Inc.
PO Box 659
Barton, VT 05822
Helping you with all your hand-paint knitting needs. Retailers, call toll-free at 800-739-7701, or please visit www.cherryyarn.com to find a retailer in your area.

Retail stores specializing in Cherry Tree Hill hand-painted yarns:

Artistic Needles
1545 Hawthorne Ave. NE
Salem, OR 97301
503-589-1502

Nancy's Knits
5266 Beechnut
Houston, TX 77096
713-661-9411

Needleworks Inc.
24 E. Green St. #5
Champaign, IL 61820
217-352-1340

Kraemer Yarn Shop
240 S. Main St.
Nazareth, PA 18064
610-759-1294